FOES IN AMBUSH

CAPT. CHARLES KING

1st WORLD
LIBRARY
Literary Society

Foes in Ambush

Charles King

© 1st World Library, 2007
PO Box 2211
Fairfield, IA 52556
www.1stworldlibrary.com
First Edition

LCCN: 2007930722

Softcover ISBN: 978-1-4218-4802-0
Hardcover ISBN: 978-1-4218-4705-4
eBook ISBN: 978-1-4218-4899-0

Purchase *"Foes in Ambush"*
as a traditional bound book at:
www.1stWorldLibrary.com/purchase.asp?ISBN=978-1-4218-4802-0

1st World Library is a literary, educational organization
dedicated to:

- Creating a free internet library of downloadable ebooks

- Hosting writing competitions and offering book publishing
  scholarships.

1st World Library Literary Society

Giving Back to the World

"If you want to work on the core problem, it's early school literacy."

- James Barksdale, former CEO of Netscape

"No skill is more crucial to the future of a child, or to a democratic and prosperous society, than literacy."

- Los Angeles Times

"Literacy... means far more than learning how to read and write... The aim is to transmit... knowledge and promote social participation."

- UNESCO

"Literacy is not a luxury, it is a right and a responsibility. If our world is to meet the challenges of the twenty-first century we must harness the energy and creativity of all our citizens."

- President Bill Clinton

"Parents should be encouraged to read to their children, and teachers should be equipped with all available techniques for teaching literacy, so the varying needs and capacities of individual kids can be taken into account."

- Hugh Mackay

I

The sun was just going down, a hissing globe of fire and torment. Already the lower limb was in contact with the jagged backbone of the mountain chain that rimmed the desert with purple and gold. Out on the barren, hard-baked flat in front of the corral, just where it had been unhitched when the paymaster and his safe were dumped soon after dawn, a weather-beaten ambulance was throwing unbroken a mile-long shadow towards the distant Christobal. The gateway to the east through the Santa Maria, sharply notched in the gleaming range, stood a day's march away,—a day's march now only made by night, for this was Arizona, and from the rising of the sun to the going down of the same anywhere south of that curdling mud-bath, the Gila, the only human beings impervious to the fierceness of its rays were the Apaches. "And they," growled the paymaster, as he petulantly snapped the lock of his little safe, "they're no more human than so many hyenas."

A big man physically was the custodian and disburser of government greenbacks,—so big that, as he stepped forth through the aperture in the hot adobe wall, he ducked his head to avert unwilling contact with its upper edge. Green-glass goggles, a broad-brimmed straw hat, a pongee shirt, loose trousers of brown linen, and dust-colored canvas shoes made up the outer man of a personality as distinctly unmilitary as it was ponderous. Slow and labored in movement, the major was correspondingly sluggish in speech. He sauntered out into the glare of the evening sunshine and became slowly conscious of a desire to swear at what he saw: that, though in a minute or two the day-god would "douse his glim" behind the black horizon, no preparation whatever had been made for a start. There stood the ambulance, every bolt and link and tire hot as a stove-lid, but not a mule in sight. Turning to his left, he strolled along towards a gap in the adobe wall, and entered the dusty interior of the corral. One of the four quadrupeds drowsing under the brush shelter languidly turned an inquiring eye and interrogative ear in his direction, and conveyed, after the manner of the mule, a suggestion as to supper. A Mexican boy sprawling in the shade of a bale of government hay, and clad in cotton shirt and trousers well-nigh as brown as the skin that peeped through occasional gaps, glanced up at him with languid interest an instant, and then resumed the more agreeable contemplation of the writhings of an impaled tarantula. Under another section of the shed two placid little burros were dreamily blinking at vacancy, their grizzled fronts expressive of that ineffable peace found only in the faces of saints and donkeys. In the middle of the enclosure a rude windlass coiled with rope stood stretching forth a decrepit lever-arm. The whippletree, dangling from the end over the beaten circular track, seemed cracked with heat and age. The stout rope that stretched tautly from the coil passed over a wooden wheel, and disappeared through a broad-framed aperture into the bowels of the earth. Close at hand in the shade of a brush-covered "leanto" hung three or four huge *ollas*, earthen water-jars, swathed in gunny sack and blanket. Beyond them, warped out of all possibility of future usefulness, stood what had once been the running gear of a California buck-board. Behind it dangled from dusty pegs portions of leather harness, which all the neat's-foot oil of the military pharmacopoeia could never again restore to softness or pliability. A newer edition of the same class of vehicle was covered by a canvas "'paulin." A huge stack of barley bags was piled at the far end of the corral, guarded from depredation (quadrupedal) by a barrier of wooden slats, mostly down, and by a tattered biped, very sound asleep.

"Where's the sergeant?" queried the paymaster, slowly, addressing no one in particular, but looking plaintively around him.

Still leaning a brown chin on a nearly black hand, and stirring up his spider with the forked stick he held in the other paw, the boy simply tilted his head towards the dark opening under the farther end of the shed, an aperture that seemed to lead to nothing but blackness beyond.

"What's he doing?"

"No sa-a-abe," drawled the boy, never lifting his handsome eyes from the joys before him.

"Why hasn't he harnessed up?"

A shrug of the shoulders was the only reply.

"Hey?"

"No sa-a-abe," slowly as before.

"What's your name?"

"Jose."

"Well, here, Jose, you go and tell him I want him."

The boy slowly pulled himself together and found his feet;

started reluctantly to obey; glanced back at his captive, now scuttling off for freedom; turned again, scotched him with his forked stick, and then with a vicious "huh!" drove the struggling Araneid into the sandy soil. This done, he lounged off towards the dark corner in the wall of the ranch and dove out of sight.

Presently there slowly issued from this recess a sturdy form in dusty blue blouse, the sleeves of which were decorated with chevrons in far-faded yellow. Under the shabby slouch hat a round, sun-blistered, freckled face, bristling with a week-old beard, peered forth at the staff official with an expression half of languid tolerance, half of mild irritation. In most perfunctory fashion the soldier just touched the hat-rim with his forefinger, then dropped the hand into a convenient pocket. It was plain that he felt but faint respect for the staff rank and station of the man in goggles and authority.

"Sergeant Feeny, I thought I told you I wanted everything ready to start at sunset."

"You did, sir, and then you undid it," was the prompt and sturdy reply.

The paymaster stood irresolute. Through the shading spectacles of green his eyes seemed devoid of any expression. His attitude remained unchanged, thumbs in the low-cut pockets of his wide-flapping trousers, shoulders meek and drooping.

"W-e-ll," he finally drawled, "you understood I wanted to get on to Camp Stoneman by sunrise, didn't you? Didn't my clerk, Mr. Dawes, tell you?"

"He did, yes, sir, and you don't want to get there no more

than I do, major. But I told you flat-footed if you let Donovan and those other men go back on the trail they'd find some excuse to stop at Ceralvo's, and, damn 'em, they've done it."

"Don't you s'pose they'll be along presently?"

"S'pose?" and the sun-blistered face of the cavalryman seemed to grow a shade redder as he echoed almost contemptuously the word of his superior. "S'pose? Why, major, look here!" And the short, swart trooper took three quick strides, then pointed through the western gap in the adobe wall to the gilded edge of the range where the sun had just slipped from view. "It's ten mile to that ridge, it's ten minutes since I got the last wig-wag of the signal-flag at the pass. They hadn't come through then. What chance is there of their getting here in time to light out at dark? You did tell me to have everything ready to start, and then you undid it by sending half the escort back. You've been here in hell's half-acre three days and I've been here three years. You've never been through Canon Diablo; I've been through a dozen times and never yet without a fight or a mighty good chance of one. Now you may think it's fun to run your head into an ambuscade, but I don't. You can get 'em too easy without trying here. I'm an old soldier, major, and too free spoken, perhaps, but I mean no disrespect, only I wish to God you'd listen to me next time."

"You wouldn't have had me leave those women in the lurch back at the crossing, would you?" queried the paymaster, half apologetically.

"Why, I don't believe that story at all," flatly answered Feeny; "it's some damned plant that fellow Donovan's springing on you,—a mere excuse to ride back so they could drink and gamble with those thugs at Ceralvo's. They've just been paid off and had no chance for any fun at all before they were ordered out on this escort duty. That money's been burning in their pockets now for three whole nights, and they just can't stand it so long as a drop of liquor's to be had by hard riding. No soldier is happy till he's dead broke, major, leastwise none I ever see."

"What makes you doubt the story, sergeant? It came straight enough."

"It came too damned straight, sir; that's just the trouble. It came straight from Chihuahua Pete's monte mill. It's only a hook to draw 'em back, and they played it on you because they saw you were new to the country and they knew I was asleep; and now, unless Lieutenant Drummond should happen in with his troop, there's no help for it but to wait for to-morrow night, and no certainty of getting away then."

"Well, if Mr. Drummond were here, don't you suppose he'd have gone or sent back to protect those people?"

"Oh, he'd have gone,—certainly,—that's his business, but it isn't yours, major. You've got government money there enough to buy up every rum-hole south of the Gila. You're expected to pay at Stoneman, Grant and Goodwin and Crittenden and Bowie, where they haven't had a cent since last Christmas and here it is the middle of May. You ought to have pushed through with all speed, so none of these jay-hawkers could get wind of your going, let alone the Apaches. Every hour you halt is clear gain to them, and here you've simply got to stay twenty-four hours all along of a cock-and-bull story about some stage-load of frightened women fifteen miles back at Gila Bend. It's a plant, major, that's what I believe."

Old Plummer kicked the toe of his shoe into the sandy soil

and hung a reflective head. "I wish you hadn't shut your eyes," he drawled at length.

"I wouldn't, sir, if I hadn't thought you'd keep yours open. You slept all night, sir, you and Mr. Dawes, while I rode alongside with finger on trigger every minute."

Absorbed in their gloomy conversation, neither man noticed that the wooden shutter in the adobe wall close at hand had been noiselessly opened from within, just an inch or two. Neither knew, neither could see that behind it, in the gathering darkness of the short summer evening, a shadowy form was crouching.

"Then you think we must stay here, do you?" queried the paymaster.

"Think? I know it. Why, the range ahead is alive with Apaches, and we can't stand 'em off with only half a dozen men. Your clerk's no 'count, major."

Old Plummer stood irresolute. His clerk, a consumptive and broken-down relative, was at that moment lying nerveless on a rude bunk within the ranch, bemoaning the fate that had impelled him to seek Arizona in search of health. He was indeed of little "'count," as the paymaster well knew. After a moment's painful thought the words rose slowly to his lips.

"Well, perhaps you know best, so here we stay till to-morrow night, or at least until they get back."

One could almost hear the whisper in the deep recess of the retaining wall,—sibilant, gasping. Some one crouching still farther back in the black depths of the interior *did* hear.

"*Santa Maria!*"

But when a moment later the proprietor of this roadside ranch, this artificial oasis in a land of desolation, strolled into the big bare room where half a dozen troopers were dozing or gambling, it was with an air of confidential joviality that he whispered to the corporal in charge,—

"Our fren', the major, he riffuse me sell you aguardiente,—mescal; but wait—to-night."

"Oh, damn it, Moreno, we'll be half-way to Stoneman by that time," interrupted the trooper, savagely. "Who's to know where we got the stuff? We'll make 'em believe Donovan's squad brought it in from Ceralvo's. Give me a drink now anyhow, you infernal Greaser; I'm all burnt out with such a day as this. We've got to start the moment they get back, and there won't be any time then."

"Hush, caballero; they come not to-night. You will rest here."

"Why, how in blazes do you know?"

"Softly!—I know not. I know noting; yet, *mira!*—I know. They talk long in the corral,—the major and that pig of a sergeant;—for him I snap my finger. Look you!" And Moreno gave a flip indicative of combined defiance and disdain.

"Don't you count on his not finding out, Moreno. It's all easy enough so far as the major's concerned, but that blackguard Feeny's different, I tell you. He'd hear the gurgle of the spigot if he were ten miles across the Gila, and be here to bust things before you could serve out a gill,—damn him! He's been keen enough to put that psalm-singing Yankee on guard over your liquor. How're you going to get at it, anyhow?"

Charles King

For all answer the Mexican placed the forefinger of his left hand upon his lips and with that of the right hand pointed significantly to the hard-beaten earthen floor.

"Ah—I have a mine," he whispered. "You will not betray, eh? Shu-u! Hush! He comes now."

The gruff voice of Sergeant Feeny broke up the colloquy.

"Corporal Murphy, take what men you have here and groom at once. Feed and water too.—Moreno, I want supper cooked for eight in thirty minutes.—Drop those cards now, you men; you should have been sleeping as I told you, so as to be ready for work to-night."

"Shure we don't go to-night, sergeant?"

"Who says that?" demanded Feeny, quickly, whirling upon his subordinates. The corporal looked embarrassed and turned to Moreno for support. Moreno, profoundly calm, was as profoundly oblivious.

"Moreno there," began Murphy, finding himself compelled to speak.

"I?" gravely, courteously protested the Mexican, with depre-catory shrug of his shoulders and upward lift of eyebrow. "I? What know I? I do but say the Corporal Donovan is not come. How know I you go not out to-night?"

"Neither you nor the likes of you knows," was Feeny's stern retort. "We go when we will and no questions asked. As for you, Murphy, you be ready, and it's me you'll ask, not any outsider, when we go. I've had enough to swear at to-day without you fellows playing off on me. Go or no go—no liquor, mind you. The first man I catch drinking I'll tie by the thumbs to the back of the ambulance, and he'll foot it to Stoneman."

No words were wasted in remonstrance or reply. These were indeed "the days of the empire" in Arizona,—days soon after the great war of the rebellion, when men drank and swore and fought and gambled in the rough life of their exile, but obeyed, and obeyed without question, the officers appointed over them. These were the days when veteran sergeants like Feeny—men who had served under St. George Cooke and Sumner and Harney on the wide frontier before the war, who had ridden with the starry guidons in many a wild, whirling charge under Sheridan and Merritt and Custer in the valley of Virginia—held almost despotic powers among the troopers who spent that enlistment in the isolation of Arizona. Rare were the cases when they abused their privilege. Stern was their rule, rude their speech, but by officers and men alike they were trusted and respected. As for Feeny, there were not lacking those who declared him spoiled. Twice that day had the paymaster been on the point of rebuking his apparent indifference. Twice had he withheld his censure, knowing, after all, Feeny to be in the right and himself in the wrong. And now in the gathering shades of night, as he stood in silence watching the brisk process of grooming, and noted how thorough and business-like, even though sharp and stern, was Feeny, the paymaster was wishing he had not ventured to disregard the caution of so skilled a veteran.

And yet the paymaster, having a human heart in his breast, had been sorely tried, for the appeal that came for help was one he could not well resist. Passing Ceralvo's at midnight and pushing relentlessly ahead instead of halting there as the men had hoped, the party was challenged in the Mexican tongue.

"*Que viene?*"

To which unlooked-for and uncalled-for demand the leading trooper, scorning Greaser interference in American territory, promptly answered,—

"Go to hell!"

All the same he heard the click of lock and was prompt to draw his own Colt, as did likewise the little squad riding ahead of the creaking ambulance. The two leaders of the mules whirled instantly about and became tangled up with the wheel team, and the paymaster was pitched out of a dream into a doubled-up mass on the opposite seat. To his startled questions the driver could only make reply that he didn't know what was the matter; the sergeant had gone ahead to see. Presently Feeny shouted "Forward!" and on they went again, and not until Ceralvo's was a mile behind could the major learn the cause of the detention. "Some of Ceralvo's people," answered Feeny, "damn their impudence! They thought to stop us and turn us in there by stories of Indian raids just below us,—three prospectors murdered twenty-four miles this side of the Sonora line. Cochises's people never came this far west of the Chiricahua Range. It's white cut-throats maybe, and we'll need our whole command."

And yet in the glaring sunshine of that May morning, after they had unsaddled at Moreno's, after the sergeant, wearied with the vigils of two successive nights, had gone to sleep in the coolest shade he could find, there came riding across the sun-baked, cactus-dotted plain at the west a young man who had the features of the American and the grave, courteous bearing of the Mexican.

"My name is Harvey," said he. "My sisters, who have been in San Francisco at school, are with me on the way to visit our parents in Tucson. Father was to have met us at the Bend with relays of mules. We have waited forty-eight hours and can wait no longer. For God's sake let half a dozen of your men ride out and escort them down here. There is no doubt in the world the Apaches are in the mountains on both sides, and I'm trembling for fear they've already found our camp. None of my party dared make the ride, so I had to come."

What was Plummer to do? He didn't want to rouse the sergeant. This wasn't going back to Ceralvo's, but riding northward to the rescue of imperilled beauty. He simply couldn't refuse, especially when Donovan and others were eager to go. From Mr. Harvey he learned that his father had married into an old Spanish Mexican family at Havana, had been induced by them to take charge of certain business in Matamoras, and that long afterwards he had removed to Guaymas and thence to Tucson. The children had been educated at San Francisco, and the sisters, now seventeen and fifteen years of age respectively, were soon to go to Cuba to visit relatives of their mother, but were determined once more to see the quaint old home at Tucson before so doing; hence this journey under his charge. The story seemed straight enough. Plummer had never yet been to Tucson, but at Drum Barracks and Wilmington he had often heard of the Harveys, and Donovan swore he knew them all by sight, especially the old man. The matter was settled before Plummer really knew whether to take the responsibility or not, and the cavalry corporal with five men rode back into the fiery heat of the Arizona day and was miles away towards the Gila before Feeny awoke to a realizing sense of what had happened. Then he came out and blasphemed. There in that wretched little green safe were locked up thousands enough of dollars to tempt all the outlawry of the Occident to any deed of desperation that might lead to the capture of the booty, and with Donovan and his party away Feeny saw he had but half a dozen men for defence.

At his interposition the major had at least done one thing,— warned Moreno not to sell a drop of his fiery mescal to any one of the men; and, when the Mexican expressed entire willingness to acquiesce, Feeny's suspicions were redoubled, and he picked out Trooper Latham, a New Englander whom some strange and untoward fate had led into the ranks, and stationed him in the bullet-scarred bar-room of the ranch, with strict orders to allow not a drop to be drawn or served to any one without the sanction of Sergeant Feeny or his superior officer, the major. Even the humiliation of this proceeding had in no wise disturbed Moreno's suavity. "All I possess is at your feet," he had said to the major, with Castilian grace and gravity; "take or withhold it as you will."

"Infernal old hypocrite!" swore Feeny, between his strong, set teeth. "I believe he'd like nothing better than to get the escort drunk and turn us over bag and baggage to the Morales gang."

Thrice during the hot afternoon had Feeny scouted the premises and striven to find what number and manner of men Moreno might have in concealment there. Questioning was of little use. Moreno was ready to answer to anything, and was never known to halt at a lie. Old Miguel, the half-breed, who did odd jobs about the well and the corral, expressed profound ignorance both of the situation and Feeny's English. The Mexican boy had but one answer to all queries: "No sa-a-abe." Other occupants there were, but these even Feeny's sense of duty could not prompt him to disturb. Somewhere in the depths of the domestic portion of the ranch, where the brush on the flat roof was piled most heavily and the walls were jealously thick, all scouting-parties or escorts well knew that Moreno's wife and daughter were hidden from prying eyes, and rumor had it that often there were more than two feminine occupants; that these were sometimes joined by three or four others,—wives or sweethearts of outlawed men who rode with Pasqual Morales, and all Arizona knew that Pasqual Morales had little more Mexican blood in his veins than had Feeny himself. He was an Americano, a cursed Gringo for whom long years ago the sheriffs of California and Nevada had chased in vain, who had sought refuge and a mate in Sonora, and whose swarthy features found no difficulty in masquerading under a Mexican name when the language of love had made him familiar with the Mexican tongue.

Slow to action, slow of speech as was the paymaster, he was not slow to see that Sergeant Feeny was anxious and ill at ease, and if a veteran trooper whom his captain had pronounced the coolest, pluckiest, and most reliable man in the regiment, could be so disturbed over the indications, it was high time to take precaution. What was the threatened danger? Apaches? They would never assault the ranch with its guard of soldiers, whatsoever they might do in the canons in the range beyond. Outlaws? They had not been heard of for months. He had inquired into all this at Yuma, at the stage stations, by mail of the commanding officers at Lowell and Bowie and Grant. Not for six months had a stage been "held up" or a buck-board "jumped" south of the turbid Gila. True, there was rumor of riot and lawlessness among the miners at Castle Dome and the customary shooting scrape at Ehrenberg and La Paz, but these were river towns, far behind him now as he looked back over the desert trail and aloft into the star-studded, cloudless sky. Nothing could be more placid, nothing less prophetic of peril or ambush than this exquisite summer night. Somewhere within the forbidden region of Moreno's harem a guitar was beginning to tinkle softly. That was all very well, but then a woman's voice, anything but soft, took up a strange, monotonous refrain. Line after line, verse after verse it ran, harsh, changeless. He could not distinguish the words,—he did not wish to; the music was bad enough in all conscience, whatsoever it might

Charles King

become when sung by youth or beauty. As it fell from the lips of Senora Moreno the air was a succession of vocal nasal disharmonies, high-pitched, strident, nerve-wracking.

Unable to listen after the third repetition, Plummer slowly retired from the corral and once more appeared at the front, just in time for a sensation. Two troopers, two of the men who had ridden back with Donovan, came lurching into the lighted space before the main entrance. At sight of the paymaster one of them stiffened up and with preternatural gravity of mien executed the salute. The other, with an envelope in his hand, reeled out of saddle, failed to catch his balance, plunged heavily into the sand and lay there. Corporal Murphy sprang eagerly forward, the first man to reach him, and turned the prostrate trooper over on his back.

"What's the matter?" queried Plummer. "Is he sick?"

"Sick is it?" was the quick retort, as the corporal sniffed at the tainted breath of the sufferer. "Be the powers! I only wish I had half his disayse."

And then came Feeny, glaring, wrathful.

"Come down off the top of that horse, Mullan," he ordered, fiercely. "How—how'd ye get here? Which way'd ye come? Where's the rest?"

With the ponderous dignity of inebriety, Mullan slowly pointed up the desert under the spot where the pole-star glowed in the northern skies.

"Sarsh'nt," he hiccoughed, "we're—we're too late; 'Paches got there—first."

"Hwat! hwat!" thundered Feeny. "D'ye mean there *were*

women,—that it wasn't a plant?"

"Fack."

"Hware's your despatches, you drunken lout? How dare you dhrink when there was fight ahead? Hware's your despatches? and may heaven blast the souls of you both!"

"Here, sergeant," said Murphy, wrenching the soiled envelope from the loose grasp of the prostrate trooper.

"It's to you, sir," said Feeny, with one glance at the sprawling superscription. "In God's name read and let us know what devil's work's abroad to-night."

Even Plummer's pudgy fingers trembled as he tore open the dingy packet. Old Moreno came forth with a light, his white teeth gleaming, his black eyes flashing from one to another of the group. Holding the pencilled page close to the lantern, the paymaster read aloud,—

"Camp burned. One man killed; others scattered; mules and buck-board gone. For God's sake help in the pursuit. Strike for Raton Pass. The Indians have run away my poor sisters.

"EDWARD HARVEY."

The major dropped the paper, fairly stunned with dismay. Feeny sprang forward, picked it up, and eagerly scrutinized the page. Mullan, standing unsteadily at the head of his wearied and dejected horse, was looking on with glassy eyes, his lips vainly striving to frame further particulars. Leaving their supper unfinished, the other men of the little squad had come tumbling out into the summer night. No one paid other heed to the trooper sprawling in the sand. Already in deep, drunken slumber, he was breathing stertorously. Feeny's eyes seemed fastened to the letter. Line by line, word by word, again and again he spelled it through. Suddenly he leaped forward and clutched Mullan at the throat, shaking him violently.

"Answer now. Hware'd you get your liquor? Didn't this fellow give it to you?"

"On my honor—no, sarsh'nt, 'pon my 'on—"

"Oh, to hell with your honor and you with it! Hware'd you get it if it wasn't from him? Shure you've not been near Ceralvo's?"

"No, sarsh'nt, no Ceralvo's. We met couple gen'l'men—perfec' gen'l'men, ranchers; they were going after the Indians. They gave us jus' o-one drink—'piece. Jus' five minutes—go."

"How far away was this? Hware were they? Answer or, damn you, I'll shake the truth out of you!" shouted Feeny, suiting action to word. "Spake before you, too, are lying like that other hog. Did you ever see the camp? Did you ever get to the crossing at all? Douse a dipper of water over him, you Latham, quick. Wake up, I say, Mullan. For the love of God, major, I believe they're both drugged. I believe it's all a damned lie. I believe it's only a skame to get you to send out the rest of your escort, so they can tackle you alone. Kick him, Murphy, kick him; throt him round; don't let him get to sleep. Answer me, you scoundrel!" he fairly yelled, for Mullan's head was drooping on his breast and every lurch promised to land him on his face. Twice his knees doubled up like a foot-rule and the stout little sergeant had to jerk him to his feet.

"Search 'em both. See if they've a flask betune 'em, Latham.

Answer me, Mullan, did you see the burned camp? Did you see the dead man? Did—Oh, murther! he's gone! There's never a word to be got out of aither of them this night. But don't you believe that letther, major. Don't you trust a word of it; it's false as hell. It's only a plant to rob ye of your escort first and your life and money later. That's it, men, douse them, kick them, murther them both if you like,—the curs!—and they'd drink when they knowed every man was needed." And adding force to his words, Feeny drove a furious kick at the luckless Mullan.

"Do you mean there is no truth in this? Do you mean you think it all a fraud, a trick?" at last queried the major. "Why, it seems incredible!"

"I say just what I mean, major. It's a plot to rob you. I mean the gang has gathered for that very purpose. I mean that every story told us about the Apaches west or south of here or between us and the Gila is a bloody lie. The guard at the signal-station hadn't seen or heard of them. They laughed at me when I told them what they tried to make us believe at Ceralvo's. 'Twas there they wanted to have you stop, for there you'd have no chance at all. Shure, do you suppose if the Apaches *were* out—if this story *was* true—they wouldn't have heard it and investigated it by this time, and the beacon-fire would have been blazing at the Picacho?"

Then Murphy turned and ran around the corner of the corral to a point where he could see the dim outline of the range against the western sky. The next moment his voice rose upon the night air, vibrant, thrilling,—

"Look! God be good to us, major! It's no lie. The signal-fire's blazing at the peak."

II

Late that night, with jaded steeds, a little troop of cavalry was pushing westward across the desert. The young May moon was sinking to rest, its pure pallid light shining faintly in contrast with the ruddy glow of some distant beacon in the mountains beneath. Ever since nightfall the rock buttress at the pass had been reflecting the lurid glare of the leaping flames as, time and again, unseen but busy hands heaped on fresh fuel and sent the sparks whirling in fiery eddies to the sky. Languid and depressed after a long day's battling with the fierce white sunshine, horses and men would gladly have spent the early hours of night dozing at their rude bivouac in the Christobal. Ever since nine in the morning, after a long night march, they had sought such shade as the burning rocks might afford, scooping up the tepid water from the natural tanks at the bottom of the canon and thanking Providence it was not alkali. The lieutenant commanding, a tall, wiry, keen-faced young fellow, had made the rounds of his camp at sunset, carefully picking up and scrutinizing the feet of his horses and sending the farrier to tack on here and there a starting shoe. Gaunt and sunburned were his short-coupled California chargers, as were their tough-looking riders; fetlocks and beards were uniformly ragged; shoes of leather and shoes of iron showed equal wear. A bronze-faced sergeant, silently following his young chief, watched him with inquiring eyes and waited for the decision that was to condemn the command to another night march across the desert, or remand them to rest until an hour or so before the dawn.

"How far did you say it was to Ceralvo's, sergeant?"

"About twenty-two miles, west."

"And to Moreno's?"

"About fifteen, sir; off here." And the sergeant pointed out across the plain, lying like a dun-colored blanket far towards the southern horizon.

"We can get barley and water at both?"

"Plenty, sir."

"The men would rather wait here, I suppose, until two or three o'clock?"

"Very much, sir; they haven't been able to rest at all to-day. I've fed out the last of the barley, though."

The lieutenant reflected a moment, pensively studying the legs of the trumpeter's horse.

"Is there any chance of Moreno's people not having heard about the Apaches in the Christobal?"

"Hardly, sir; they are nearer the Tucson road than we are. The stage must have gone through this morning early. It's nothing new anyhow. I've never known the time when the Indians were not in the neighborhood of that range. Moreno, too, is an old hand, sir."

The lieutenant looked long and intently out over the dreary flats beyond the foot-hills. Like the bottom of some prehistoric lake long since sucked dry by the action of the sun, the parched earth stretched away in mile after mile of monotonous, life-ridden desert, a Sahara without sign of an oasis, a sandy barren shunned even by scorpion and centipede. Already the glow was dying from the western sky. The red rim of the distant range was purpling. The golden gleam that flashed from rock to rock as the sun went down had vanished from all but the loftiest summits, and deep, dark shadows were creeping slowly out across the plain. Over the great expanse not so much as the faintest spark could be seen. Aloft, the greater stars were beginning to peep through the veil of pallid blue, while over the distant pass the sun's fair hand-maiden and train-bearer, with slow, stately mien, was sinking in the wake of her lord, as though following him to his rest. Not a breath of air was astir. The night came on still as the realms of solitude. Only the low chatter of the men, the occasional stamp of iron-shod hoof or the munching jaws of the tired steeds broke in upon the perfect silence. From their covert in the westward slope of the Christobal the two sentries of the little command looked out upon a lifeless world. Beneath them, whiffing their pipes after their frugal supper, the troopers were chatting in low tone, some of them already spreading their blankets among the shelving rocks. The embers from the cook fire glowed a deeper red as the darkness gathered in the pass, and every man seemed to start as though stung with sudden spur when sharp, quick, and imperative there came the cry from the lips of the farther sentry,—

"Fire, sir,—out to the west!"

In an instant Lieutenant Drummond had leaped down the rocky canon and, field-glass in hand, was standing by the sentry's side. No need to question "Where away?" Far out across the intervening plain a column of flame was darting upward, gaining force and volume with every moment. The lieutenant never even paused to raise the glass to his eyes. No magnifying power was needed to see the distant pyre; no prolonged search to tell him what was meant. The troopers who had sprung to their feet and were already eagerly following turned short in their tracks at his first word.

"Saddle up, men. It's the beacon at Signal Peak."

Then came a scene of bustle. No words were spoken; no further orders given. With the skill of long practice the men gathered their few belongings, shook out the dingy horse-blankets and then, carefully folding, laid them creaseless back of the gaunt withers of their faithful mounts. The worn old saddles were deftly set, the crude buckles of the old days, long since replaced by cincha loop, snapped into place; lariats coiled and swung from the cantle-rings; dusty old bits and bridles adjusted; then came the slipping into carbine-slings and thimble-belts, the quick lacing of Indian moccasin or canvas legging, the filling of canteens in the tepid tanks below, while all the time the cooks and packers were flying about gathering up the pots and pans and storing rations, bags, and blankets on the roomy *apparejos*. Drummond was in the act of swinging into saddle when his sergeant hastened up.

"Beg pardon, lieutenant, but shall I leave a small guard with the pack-train or can they come right along?"

"They'll go with us, of course. We can't leave them here. We must head for Ceralvo's at once. How could those Indians have got over that way?"

"It is beyond me to say, sir. I didn't know they ever went west of the Santa Maria."

"I can hardly believe it now, but there's no doubting that signal; it is to call us thither at all speed wherever we may be, and means only one thing,—'Apaches here.' Sergeant Wing is not the man to get stampeded. Can they have jumped the stage, do you think, or attacked some of Ceralvo's people?"

"Lord knows, sir. I don't see how they could have swung around there; there's nothing to tempt them along that range until they get to the pass itself. They must have come around south of Moreno's."

"I think not, sergeant."

The words were spoken in a very quiet voice. Drummond turned in surprise, his foot in the stirrup, and looked at the speaker, a keen-eyed trooper of middle age, whose hair was already sprinkled with gray.

"Why not, Bland?"

"Because we have been along the range for nearly fifty miles below here, sir, and haven't crossed a sign, and because I understand now what I couldn't account for at two o'clock,— what I thought must be imagination."

"What was that?"

"Smoke, sir, off towards the Gila, north of Ceralvo's, I should say, just about north of west of where we are."

"Why didn't you report it?"

"You were asleep, sir, and by the time I got the glasses and looked it had faded out entirely; but it's my belief the Indians are between us and the river, or were over there north of

Ceralvo's to-day. If not Indians, who?"

"You ride with me, Bland. I'll talk with you further about this. Come on with the men as soon as you have the packs ready, sergeant." And so saying, Lieutenant Drummond mounted and rode slowly down the winding trail among the boulders. At the foot of the slope, where the water lay gleaming in its rocky bed, he reined his horse to the left to give him his fill of the pool, and here the trooper addressed as Bland presently joined him.

"Where was it you enlisted, Bland?" was the younger soldier's first question. "I understand you are familiar with all this country."

"At Tucson, sir, six months ago, after the stage company discharged me."

"I remember," was the answer, as the lieutenant gently drew rein to lift his horse's head. "I think you were so frank as to give the reason of your quitting their employment."

"Well, there was no sense trying to conceal it, or anything else a man may do out here, lieutenant. They fired me for drinking too much at the wrong time. The section boss said he couldn't help himself, and I don't suppose he could."

"As I remember," said Drummond, presently, and with hesitation, for he hated to pry into the past of a man who spoke so frankly and who made no effort to conceal his weakness, "you were driver of the buck-board the Morales gang held up last November over near the Catarinas."

"Yes; that's the time I got drunk, sir. It's all that saved me from being killed, and between keeping sober and losing my life or getting drunk and losing a job, I preferred the latter."

"Yet you were in a measure responsible for the safety of your passengers and mail, were you not?"

"Well, no, sir, not after the warning I gave the company. I told them Ramon Morales was in Tucson the night before we had to pull out, and wherever he was that infernal cut-throat of a brother of his wasn't far away. I told them it was taking chances to let Judge Gillette and that infantry quartermaster try to go through without escort. I begged to throw up the job that very night, but they held me to my contract, and I had to go. We were jumped not ten miles out of town, and before any one could draw a Derringer every man of us was covered. The judge might have known they'd shoot him on sight ever since that Greaser from Hermosillo was lynched. But they never harmed the quartermaster."

"Huh! The devil they didn't!" laughed the lieutenant. "They took his watch and his money and everything he had on except his underclothing. How long had you been driving when that happened?"

"Just eight months, sir, between Tucson and Grant."

"And did you never serve with the cavalry before? You ride as though you had."

"Most men hereabouts served on one side or other," said Bland, calmly, as his horse finished his long pull at the water.

"And your side was—?"

"Confederate," was the brief reply. "I was born in Texas. Here comes the troop, sir."

"Come on, then. I want to ask you about that trail to

Crittenden as we ride. We make first for the Picacho Pass from here."

"Why, that's south of west, sir," answered Bland. "I had thought perhaps the lieutenant would want to go northward towards the Gila to head off any parties of the Apaches that might be striving to get away eastward with their booty. They must have picked up something over at the Bend."

"They're more likely to go southward, Bland, for they know where we've been scouting all the week. No, I'll march straight to the signal. There they must know where the Indians have gone."

"Ay, ay, sir, but then you can only pursue, and a stern chase is a long one."

Drummond turned in saddle as they rode forth upon the dark *falda* and gazed long and fixedly at the trooper by his side. Imperturbably Bland continued to look straight ahead. Queer stories had been afloat regarding this new acquisition. He mingled but little with the men. He affected rather the society of the better class of non-commissioned officers, an offence not likely to be condoned in a recruit. He was already distinguished for his easy mastery of every detail of a cavalryman's duty, and for his readiness to go at any or all times on scout, escort, or patrol, and the more hazardous or lonely the task the better he seemed to like it. Then he was helpful about the offices in garrison, wrote a neat hand, was often pressed into service to aid with the quartermaster or commissary papers, and had been offered permanent daily duty as company clerk, but begged off, saying he loved a horse and cavalry work too well to be mured in an office. He was silence and reticence itself on matters affecting other people, but the soul of frankness, apparently, where he was personally concerned. Anybody was welcome to know his past, he said. He was raised in Texas; had lived for years on the frontier; had been through Arizona with a bull-team in the 50's, and had 'listed under the banner of the Lone Star when Texas went the way of all the sisterhood of Southern (not border) States, and then, being stranded after the war, had "bullwhacked" again through New Mexico; had drifted again across the Mimbres and down to the old Spanish-Mexican town of Tucson; had tried prospecting, mail-riding, buck-board driving, gambling; had been one of the sheriff's posse that cleaned out Sonora Bill's little band of thugs and cut-throats, and had expressed entire willingness to officiate as that lively outlaw's executioner in case of his capture. He had twice been robbed while driving the stage across the divide and had been left for dead in the Maricopa range, an episode which he said was the primal cause of his dissipations later. Finally, after a summary discharge he had come to the adjutant at Camp Lowell, presented two or three certificates of good character and bravery in the field from officers who bore famous names in the Southern army, and the regimental recruiting officer thought he could put up with an occasional drunk in a man who promised to make as good a trooper under the stars and stripes as he had made under the stars and bars. And so he was enlisted, and, to the surprise of everybody, hadn't taken a drop since.

Now this, said the rank and file, was proof positive of something radically wrong, either in his disposition or his record. It was entirely comprehensible and fully in accordance with human nature and the merits of the case that a man should quit drinking when he quit the army, but that a man with the blot of an occasional spree on his escutcheon should enlist for any other cause than sheer desperation, and should then become a teetotaler, was nothing short of *prima facie* evidence of moral depravity.

"There's something behind it all, fellers," said Corporal

Murphy, "and I mean to keep an eye on him from this out. If he don't dhrink next pay-day, look out for him. He's a professional gambler laying for your hard-earned greenbacks."

And so while the seniors among the sergeants were becoming gradually the associates, if not the intimates, of this fine-looking trooper, the mass of the regiment, or rather the little detachment thereof stationed at Lowell, looked upon Bland with the eye of suspicion. There was one sergeant who repudiated him entirely, and who openly professed his disbelief in Bland's account of himself, and that was Feeny. "He may have testimonials from all Texas," said he, hotly, "but I've no use for that sort of credentials. Who can vouch for his goings and comings hereabouts before he joined us? I think Murphy's right, and if I was stationed at Lowell and belonged to his troop, you bet I'd watch him close."

Now, in all the command it would have been a hard matter to find a soldier in whose favor appearances were so unanimously allied. Tall, erect, sinewy, and active, he rode or walked with an easy grace that none could fail to mark. His features were fine and clear cut; his eyes a dark hazel, with heavy curling lashes and bushy, low-arched brows; his complexion, naturally dark, was bronzed by sun and sand-storm to a hue almost Mexican. He shaved clean all but the heavy moustache that drooped over his firm lips, and the sprinkling of gray about the brows, temples, and moustache was most becoming to his peculiar style. One prominent mark had he which the descriptive book of his company referred to simply as "sabre-scar on right jaw," but it deserved mention more extended, for the whitish streak ran like a groove from just below the ear-tip to the angle of the square, resolute chin. It looked as though in some desperate fray a mad sweep had been made with vengeful blade straight for the jugular, and, just missing that, had laid open the jaw for full four inches. "But," said Feeny, "what could he have been doing, and in what position could he have been, sitting or standing, to get a sabre-stroke like that? Where was his guard? A Bowie-knife, now—" and there the suggestion ended.

But it was the scarred side of Bland's soldierly face that young Lieutenant Drummond was so closely studying as they rode out into the starlit Arizona night. He, too, had heard the camp chat about this apparently frank, open-hearted trooper, and had found himself more than once speculating as to his real past, not the past of his imagination or of his easy off-hand description. By this time, in perfect silence save for the occasional clink of canteen, the gurgle of imprisoned water, or, once in a while, the click of iron-shod hoof, the troop was marching in shadowy column of twos well out beyond the *falda* and over the almost dead level of the plain. Far ahead the beacon still blazed brightly and beckoned them on. It was time for precaution.

"Sergeant," said Drummond, "send a corporal and four men forward. Let them spread out across the front and keep three or four hundred yards ahead of us. Better take those with the freshest horses, as I want them to scout thoroughly and to be on the alert for the faintest sound. Any of our men who know this valley well?"

"None better than Bland here, sir," was the half-hesitant reply.

"W-e-l-l, I need Bland just now. Put some of the old hands and older heads on, and don't let anything escape their notice."

"Beg pardon, lieutenant, but what's to be the line of direction? When we started it was understood that we were to take the shortest cut for Ceralvo's, and now we're heading for the Picatch."

"No, we make for the pass first; that's the quickest way to reach the signal-station, then we learn where to strike for the Indians. Did you ever hear of their being as far west as the Maricopa range before?"

"Never, sir, in the whole time we've been here, and since the lieutenant joined they've never been heard of crossing the Santa Maria valley."

"What on earth could tempt them out so far? There's nothing to be gained and every chance of being cut off by troops from Grant and Bowie, even if they do succeed in slipping by us."

"That's more than I can tell, sir. The men say the paymaster's coming along this week; they heard it from the quartermaster's train we passed at the Cienega three days ago."

Trooper Bland was riding in silence on the left of the detachment commander as he had been directed. The sergeant had come up on the other flank.

"What men heard this?" asked Drummond, quickly.

"Why, Patterson told me, sir, and Lucas and Quinn, and I think Bland here was talking with the train escort and must have heard it."

"Did you, Bland?" asked the lieutenant, as he whirled suddenly in his saddle and faced the trooper.

"Yes, sir," was the prompt reply; "several of the men spoke of it. It's about the most welcome piece of news they could give to fellows who had four months' pay due."

In the isolation of this mountain scouting business, when, as often happens, one officer is out alone for weeks with no comrades or associates but his detachment, it naturally results that a greater freedom of intercourse and speech is developed between the commander and some, at least, of his party than would ever be the case in years of garrison life; and so it happened that for the moment Drummond forgot the commander in the man.

"It is most extraordinary," he said, "that just when a paymaster is anxious to keep secret the date and route of his coming the whole thing is heralded ahead. We have no telegraph, and yet three days ago we knew that Major Plummer was starting on his first trip. He ought to have been at Ceralvo's last night. By Jupiter! suppose he *was*—and had but a small escort? What else could that signal-fire mean? Here! get those men out to the front now at once; we must push ahead for all we're worth."

And so at midnight, with steeds panting and jaded, with the pass and the Picacho only four miles ahead, the little detachment was tripping noiselessly through the darkness, and, all alert and eager, Drummond was riding midway between his scouts and the main body so that no sound close at hand might distract his attention from hails or signals farther out. Suddenly he heard an exclamation ahead, the snort of a frightened horse, then some muffled objurgations, a rider urging a reluctant steed to approach some suspicious object, and, spurring his own spirited charger forward, Mr. Drummond came presently upon the corporal just dismounting in the darkness and striving to lead his boon companion, whom he could not drive, up to some dark object lying on the plain. This, too, failed. A low whistle, however, brought one of the other scouts trotting in to the rescue.

"Hold him a minute, Burke," said the corporal, handing up the reins. "There's something out here this brute shied at and I can't get him near it again." With that he pushed out to the front while the others listened expectant. A moment later a match was struck, and presently burned brightly in the black and breathless night. Then came the startled cry,—

"My God! lieutenant. It's Corporal Donovan and his horse,—both dead."

And even there Mr. Drummond noted that Bland was about the first of the column to come hurrying forward to the scene.

Ten minutes' investigation threw but little light upon the tragedy. Some stumps of candles were found in the saddle-bags and packs, and with these the men scoured the plain for signs. Spreading well out from the centre, they closely examined the sandy level. From the north came the trail of two cavalry horses, shod alike, both at the lope, both draggy and weary. From the point where lay Donovan and his steed there was but one horse-track. Whirling sharply around, the rider had sent his mount at thundering gallop back across the valley; then a hundred yards away, in long curve, had reined him to the southeast. The troopers who followed the hoof-marks out about an eighth of a mile declared that, unwounded, both horse and rider were making the best of their way towards Moreno's ranch. Farther search, not fifty yards to the front, revealed the fact that at the edge of a little depression and behind some cactus-bushes three human forms had been lying prone, and from this point probably had sped the deadly bullet.

"Apaches, by God!" muttered one of the men.

"Apaches, your grandmother!" was the sergeant's fierce

reply. "Will you never learn sense, Moore? When did Apaches take to wearing store clothes and heeled boots? There's no Apache in this, lieutenant. Look here, sir, and here. Move out farther, some of you fellows, and see where they hid their horses. Corporal Donovan was with 'C' troop down the Gila last week, sir. They were to meet and escort the paymaster most like. It's my belief he was one of the guard, and that the ambulance has been jumped this very night. These are road agents, not Apaches, and God knows what's happened if they've got away with Patsy. Sure he was one of the nerviest men in the whole troop, sir."

Drummond listened, every nerve a-tingle, even while with hurried hands he cut open the shirt at the brawny throat and felt for fluttering heart-beat or faintest sign of life. Useless. The shot-hole under the left eye told plainly that the leaden missile had torn its way through the brain and that death must have been instantaneous. The soldier's arms and accoutrements, the horse's equipments, were gone. The bodies lay unmutilated. The story was plain. Separated in some way from the detachment, Donovan and his companion had probably sighted the signal blazing at the pass and come riding hard to reach the spot, when the unseen foe crouching across their path had suddenly fired the fatal shots. Now, where was the paymaster? Where the escort? Where the men who fed the signal-fire,—the fire that long before midnight had died utterly away. Whither should the weary detachment direct its march? Ceralvo's lay a dozen miles off to the northwest, Moreno's perhaps eight or nine to the southeast. Why had the escaped trooper headed his fleeing steed in that direction? Had there been pursuit? Ay, ten minutes' search over the still and desolate plain revealed the fact that two horsemen lurking in a sand-pit or dry arroyo had pushed forth at top speed and ridden away full tilt across the desert, straight as the crow flies, towards Moreno's well. Even while Drummond, holding brief consultation with his sergeant, was deliberating whether to turn thither or to push for the signal-peak and learn what he could from the little squad of blue jackets there on duty, the matter was decided for him. Sudden and shrill there came the cry from the outskirts of the now dismounted troop clustered about the body of their comrade.

"Another fire, lieutenant! Look!—out here towards the Santa Maria."

The sergeant sprang to his feet, shouldering his burly way through the excited throng. One moment more and his voice was heard in louder, fiercer tones.

"No signal this time, sir. By God! they've fired Moreno's ranch!"

III

Shortly after sunset on this same hot evening the sergeant in charge of the little signal-party at the Picacho came strolling forth from his tent puffing at a battered brier-root pipe. Southward and a few hundred feet below his perch the Yuma road came twisting through the pass, and then disappeared in the gathering darkness across the desert plain that stretched between them and the distant Santa Maria. Over to the east the loftiest crags of the Christobal were still faintly tinged by the last touch of departed day. Southward still, beyond the narrow and tortuous pass, the range rose high and precipitous, covered and fringed with black masses of cedar, stunted pine, and juniper. North of west, on the line of the now invisible road, and far out towards the Gila, a faint light was just twinkling. There lay Ceralvo's, and nowhere else, save where the embers of the cook fire still glowed in a deep crevice among the rocks, was there light of any kind to be seen. A lonely spot was this in which to spend one's days, yet the soldier in charge seemed in no wise oppressed with sense of isolation. It was his comrade, sitting moodily on a convenient rock, elbows on knees and chin deep buried in his brown and hairy hands, who seemed brooding over the desolation of his surroundings.

Watching him in silence a moment, a quiet smile of amusement on his lips, Sergeant Wing sauntered over and placed a friendly hand on the broad blue shoulder.

"Well, Pikey, are you wishing yourself back in Frisco?"

"I'm wishing myself in Tophet, sergeant; it may be hotter, but it isn't as lonely as this infernal hole."

"No, it's populous enough, probably," was the response, "and," added he, with a whimsical smile, "no doubt you've lots of friends there, Pike."

"Maybe I have, and maybe I haven't. At all events, I've none here. Why in thunder couldn't you let me look into that business over at Ceralvo's instead of Jackson?—he gets everything worth having. I'm shelved for his sake day after day."

"Couldn't send *you*, Pike, on any such quest as that. Those Greasers have sharp eyes, and one look at your face would convince them that we'd lost our grip or were in for a funeral. Jackson, now, rides in as blithe as a May morning,—a May morning out of Arizona, I mean. They never get the best of him. The only trouble is he stays too long; he ought to be back here now."

"Humph! he'll be apt to come back in a hurry with Pat Donovan and those 'C' troop fellows spending their money like water at Ceralvo's."

"You still insist they're over there, do you, Pike? I think they're not. I flagged old Feeny half an hour ago that they hadn't come through here."

"Who was that fellow who rode back here with the note?" asked Pike.

"I don't know his name. 'Dutchy' they call him in 'C' troop. He's on his second enlistment."

"More fool he! The man who re-enlists in this Territory must be either drunk or Dutch." And Pike relapsed into gloomy silence again, his eyes fixed upon the faint flicker of the bar lights at Ceralvo's miles away; but Wing only laughed again, and, still puffing away at his pipe, went on down the winding trail to where in the deep shelter of the rocky walls a pool of water lay gleaming. Here he threw himself flat and, laying aside his precious pipe, drank long and eagerly; then with sudden plunge doused his hot face in the cooling flood and came up dripping.

"Thank the Lord I have no desert march to make to-day,—all on a wild-goose chase," was his pious ejaculation. "What on earth could have induced the paymaster to send a detachment over to the Gila?" He took from his pocket a pencilled note and slowly twisted it in his fingers. It was too dark to read, but in its soldierly brevity he almost knew it by heart. "The major sent Donovan with half the escort back to the Gila on an Apache scare this morning. They will probably return your way, empty-handed. Signal if they have passed. Latham knows your code and we have a good glass. Send man to Ceralvo's with orders for them to join at once if they haven't come, and flag or torch when they pass you. It's my belief they've gone there." This was signed by Feeny, and over and again had Wing been speculating as to what it all meant. When the escort with the ambulance and paymaster went through before the dawn, Feeny had roused him to ask if anything had been heard of Indians on the war-path between them and the Sonora line, and the answer was both prompt and positive, "No." As for their being north or north of west of his station, and up towards the Gila, Wing scouted the suggestion. He wished, however, that Jackson were back with such tidings as he had picked up at Ceralvo's. It was always best to be prepared, even though this was some distance away from the customary raiding-ground of the tribe.

Just then there came a hail from aloft. Pikey was shouting.

"All right," answered Wing, cheerily; "be there in a minute," and then went springing up the trail as though the climb of four hundred feet were a mere bagatelle. "What's up?— Jackson here?" he asked, short of breath as he reached the little nook in which their brush-covered tents were pitched. There was no reply.

"Pike. Oh-h, Pike! Where are you?" he called.

And presently, faint and far somewhere down in the dark canon to the south, a voice replied,—

"Down hyar. Something's coming up the road."

Surely enough. Probably a quarter-mile away a dim light as of a swinging lantern could be seen following the winding of the rough and rock-ribbed road. Then came the click of iron-shod hoofs, the crack of the long mule-whip, and a resonant imprecation in Spanish levelled at the invisible draught animals. Bounding lightly down the southward path, Sergeant Wing soon reached the roadside, and there found Pike in converse with a brace of horsemen.

"It's old Harvey's outfit, from Yuma, making for Moreno's," vouchsafed the soldier.

"Oh, is that you, Sergeant Wing? I ought to have known you were here. I'm Ned Harvey." And the taller horseman held out a hand, which Wing grasped and shook with cordial fervor.

"Which way, Mr. Harvey, and who are with you?"

"Home to Tucson. My sisters are in the Concord behind us, going to visit the old folks for a few weeks before their trip to Cuba."

"You don't tell me!" exclaimed Wing. "They're the first ladies to pass through here since I came on duty at the station two months ago. You stay at Moreno's, I suppose?"

"Yes; the governor meets us there with relays and four or five men. We knew there would be no danger west of the Santa Maria."

"W-e-ll,—did you stop at Ceralvo's or see any of their people?"

"No, I never put in there. Father's very suspicious of that gang. Why do you ask, though?"

Wing hesitated. "There was some story afloat about Apaches," he finally said. "The paymaster's escort threw off a detachment towards the Gila this morning, and I sent one of my two men back to Ceralvo's to inquire. You must have met him."

"No, we made a circuit,—came by the old trail around the head of the slough. We haven't passed anybody, have we, Tony?" he asked of the silent horseman by his side.

"None, senor; but there were many hoof-trails leading to Ceralvo's," was the answer, in the Spanish tongue.

"Then you'll need water here, Mr. Harvey. It's a ten-mile pull across to Moreno's," said Wing, as the four-mule team came laboring up to the spot and willingly halted, the lantern at the forward axle slowly settling into inertia from its pendulum-like swing.

"Where are we, Ned?" hailed a blithe young voice. Sweet and silvery it sounded to the trooper's unaccustomed ears. "Surely not at Moreno's yet?"

"Not yet, Paquita mia. Is Ruth awake? Tell her to poke that curly pate of hers out of the door. I want you to know Mr. Wing, Sergeant Wing, who has charge of the signal-station here."

Almost instantly a slender hand, holding a little brass hurricane lantern, appeared at the opening, followed by a sweet, smiling face, while just behind it peered another, only a trifle older and more serious, yet every whit as pretty. Wing raised his old felt hat and mentally cursed the luck that had sent him down there in his ragged shirt-sleeves. Pike, the cynic, busied himself in getting the buckets from underneath the stout spring wagon, and bumped his head savagely against the trunk-laden boot as he emerged.

"I never dreamed of seeing ladies to-night," laughed the sergeant. "It's the rarest sight in all the world here; but I remember you well when you came to Yuma last year. That was when you were going to school at San Francisco, I believe."

"That was when I was in short dresses and a long face, sergeant," merrily answered the younger girl. "I hated the idea of going there to school. Fan, here, was willing enough, but I had never known anything but Arizona and Mexico. All I could think of was that I was leaving home."

"She was soon reconciled, Mr. Wing," said Miss Harvey; "there were some very pleasant people on the steamer."

"Oh, very pleasant for you, Fan, but what did they care for a chit of fourteen? *You* had lovely times, of course."

"So did you, Ruth, from the very day Mr. Drummond helped you to catch your dolphin."

"Ah! we were more than half-way to San Francisco then," protested Miss Ruth, promptly, "and nobody had taken any notice of me whatever up to that minute."

"Well, Mr. Drummond made up for lost time from that on," laughed the elder sister. "I never told of her, Ned,—wasn't I good?—but Ruth lost her young heart to a cavalry cadet not a year out of the Point."

"Is it our Lieutenant Drummond who was with you?" queried Wing.

"Oh, yes; why, to be sure, he *is* of your regiment. He was going back to testify before some court at the Presidio, and—wasn't madame mean?—she wouldn't allow him to call on Ruth at the school, even when I promised to play chaperon and insure strict propriety and no flirting."

Ruth Harvey had, with quick movement, uplifted a little hand to silence her sister, but the hand dropped, startled, and the color rushed to her face at Wing's next words.

"Then you're almost sure to meet the lieutenant to-night or to-morrow. He's been scouting the Santa Maria and the Christobal and is due along here at this very moment."

And now Miss Harvey had the field to herself, for the younger sister drew back into the dark depths of the covered wagon and spoke no more. In ten minutes the team was rattling down the eastward slope, and Sergeant Wing turned with a sigh, as at last even the sound of hoof and wheel had died away. Slowly he climbed the steep and crooked trail to their aerie at the peak. No sign of Jackson yet, no message from the ranch, no signal-fires at Moreno's or beyond. Yet, was he right in telling Harvey with such precious freight to push on across that open plain when there was even rumor of Apache in the air? The loveliness of those two dark, radiant faces, the pretty white teeth flashing in the lantern light, the soft, silvery, girlish voices, the kindly, cordial hand-clasp vouchsafed him by the elder, as they rolled away,—these were things to stir the heart of any man long exiled in this desert land. It had been his custom to spend an hour in chat with his comrades before turning in for the night; but with Jackson still away and Pike still plunged in gloom, with, moreover, new and stirring emotions to investigate and analyze, Wing strolled off by himself, passed around the rocky buttress at the point and came to the broad ledge overlooking the eastward way to the distant range. Here a mass of tinder, dry baked by weeks' exposure to the burning sunshine, stood in a pyramid of firewood ready to burst in flame at first touch of the torch. Close at hand were the stacks of reserve fuel. "Never light this until you know the Indians are raiding west of the Christobal," were his orders. But well he knew that once ignited it could be seen for many a league. Here again he filled his faithful pipe and, moving safe distance away, lighted its charge and tossed the match-stump among the jagged rocks below. He saw the spark go sailing downward, unwafted from its course by faintest breath of air. Then he heard Pike's growl or something like it, and called to him to ask if he heard Jackson. No answer. Sure that he had heard the gruff, though inarticulate, voice of his comrade, he hailed again more loudly than before, and still there came no reply. Surprised, he stepped quickly back around the rocky point to where the tents lay under the sheltering cliff, and came face to face with three dark, shadowy forms, whose moccasined footsteps gave no sound, whose masked and blackened faces defied recognition, whose cocked revolvers were thrust into his very face before a lariat settled over his shoulders, snapped into place, and, yelling for help when help was miles beyond range of his ringing voice, Sergeant Wing was jerked violently to earth, dragged into a tent, strapped to a cot, deftly gagged, and then left to himself. An instant later the Picacho was lighted up with a lurid, unearthly glare; the huge column of sparks went whirling and hissing up on high, and, far and near, the great beacon was warning all seers that the fierce Apache was out in force and raiding the Yuma road.

Away out across the desert its red glare chased the Concord wagon wherein, all unconscious of the danger signal, the sisters were now chatting in low tone.

"Drive your best," had Harvey muttered to his Mexican Jehu, as he leaned out of the saddle to reach his ear. "Not a word to alarm the girls," he cautioned his companion, "but be ready for anything."

Far out beyond the swaying, bounding vehicle; far out across the blistered plain, the glare and gleam fell full upon the brown adobe walls at Moreno's, and glittering eyes and swarthy faces peered through the westward aperture, while out in the corral the night lights were dancing to and fro, and Feeny, sore perplexed, but obedient to orders, was hurrying the preparations of his men. Murphy's wild announcement had carried conviction to the major's soul, despite all Feeny's pleadings, and the sight of that beacon furiously burning, the thought of those helpless women being borne off into the horrors of captivity among the Indians, had conspired to rouse the paymaster to unlooked-for assertion of himself and his authority. In vain had Feeny begged him to think of his money, to remember that outlaws would resort to any trick to rob him of his guard, and might have even overpowered

Wing and his party and then lighted the beacon. The chain of evidence, the straight story told by his morning visitor, the awful news contained in the pencilled note brought in by Mullan, were considerations too potent to be slighted. In vain did Feeny point out to him that if Apaches were really in the neighborhood Wing would not be content with starting the fire, but would surely signal whither to go in search of them, and that no vestige of signal-torch had appeared. Old Plummer vowed he could never again know a moment of peace if he neglected to do anything or everything in his power to save the girls. Most reluctantly he agreed that Feeny should remain in charge of the safe and the two drugged and helpless men. Murphy and all the others were ordered out forthwith to march rapidly northeastward until they struck the trail of the pursuit and then to follow that. In fifteen minutes, with four pack-mules ambling behind, away they went into the darkness, and all that was left to man the ranch and defend the government treasury against all comers was the phlegmatic but determined paymaster, his physically wrecked but devoted clerk, Sergeant Feeny, raging at heart but full of fight, and a half-breed packer named Pedro; the two senseless and drunken troopers were of course of no use to anybody.

Even as the detachment mounted, Latham with it, old Moreno appeared at the door-way shrouded in his *serape*. Approaching Murphy by the side farthest from Plummer and the sergeant, he slipped a fat canteen from under his cloak and thrust it into the corporal's ready hand.

"Hush-h,—no words," he whispered. "All is well. I keep my promise." And so saying he had slunk away; but Feeny was on the off side quick as a shot, quicker than the corporal could stow the bulky vessel in his saddle-bags. Wresting it from the nerveless hand of his junior, Feeny hurled it with all his force after the Mexican's retreating form. It struck

Moreno square in the back of the neck and sent him pitching heavily forward. Only by catching at a horse-post did he save himself from a fall, but, as he straightened up, his face was one not to be looked at without a shudder; grinding teeth, snapping, flashing eyes, vengeful contortions of brow and jaw, hate, fury, and revenge, all were quivering with the muscles under that swarthy skin, and the gleaming knife was clasped in his upraised hand as, driving into the ranch and out of sight of the hated "Gringos," he burst into the room where sat his wife and daughter, and raging aloud, through that he leaped like a panther to another door, fastened on the farther side, where one instant he stood before admission could be gained, and through a panel in which there warily peered a bearded face, swarthy as his own. And then Senora Moreno hurriedly banged the shutter and took up her guitar. Something had to be done to hush the uproar of blasphemy and imprecation, mingling with the shout of exultation that instantly followed her lord's admission to the den.

Nine o'clock came. Murphy and his party were gone. The beacon still blazed at the westward pass. The twang of the guitar had ceased. Silence reigned about the ranch. Old Plummer with anxious face plodded slowly up and down the open space in front of the deserted bar. Feeny, with three loaded carbines close at hand and his belt bristling with revolvers, was dividing his attention between the safe and the still sleeping troopers. Every once in a while he would station the major at the safe, which had been hauled into the easternmost of the rooms that opened to the front instead of on the corral, and, revolver in hand, would patrol the premises, never failing to stop at a certain window behind which he believed Moreno to be lurking, to warn that impulsive Greaser not to show his head outside his room if he didn't want it blown off his shoulders; never failing on his return to stir up both recumbent forms with angry foot, and then to shower in equal portions cold water and hot imprecations upon them. To Pedro he had intrusted the duty of caring for the horses of his prostrate comrades. Every faculty he possessed was on the alert, watching for the faintest sign of treachery or hostility from within, listening with dread but stern determination for the first sound of hoof-beats from without. It must have been about ten o'clock when, leaving Mr. Dawes, the clerk, seated in the dark interior beside the safe, Feeny stepped forth to make another round, stopped to look at Mullan and his partner, now beginning to twitch uneasily and moan and toss in their drunken sleep, and then turned to seek the paymaster. Whatsoever lights Moreno had been accustomed to burn by way of lure or encouragement to belated travellers, all was gloom to-night. The bar was silence and darkness. The bare east room adjoining the corral was tenanted now only by the clerk and the precious iron box of "greenbacks." No glimmer of lamp showed there. The westward apartments, opening only one into another and thence into the corral, were still as the night, and even when a shutter was slowly pushed from within, as though the occupants craved more air, no gleam of light came through.

"Don't show your ugly mug out here, Moreno," cautioned Feeny for the fourth or fifth time, "and warn any damned cut-throat with you to keep in hiding. The man who attempts to come out gets a bullet through him."

There had been shrill protestation in Mexican Spanish and Senora Moreno's strident tones when first he conveyed his orders to the master of the ranch, but Moreno himself had made no audible reply, and, as was conjectured, had enjoined silence on his wife, for after that outbreak she spoke no more.

"I've got this approach covered anyhow," muttered the veteran. "Now if I only had men to watch those doors into the corral, I could pen Moreno and whatever he has here at his back. It's that gang of hell-hounds we passed at Ceralvo's that will pay us a call before morning, or I'm a duffer."

Once again he found the paymaster wearily, anxiously patrolling his self-assumed post out beyond the westward wall. The presence of common danger, the staff official's forgetfulness of self and his funds in his determination to aid the wretched women whom he firmly believed to have been run off by the Apaches, had won from the sergeant the tribute of more respectful demeanor, even though he held the story of the raid to be an out-and-out lie.

"Any signs or sounds yet, sir?" he questioned in muffled tone.

"Why, I thought—just a moment ago—I heard something like the crack of a whip far out there on the plain."

"That's mighty strange, sir; no stage is due coming east until to-morrow night, and no stage would dare pull out on this stretch in face of the warning there at Picacho."

"Well, it may have been imagination. My nerves are all unused to this sort of thing. How do you work this affair when you want to reload, sergeant? I'm blessed if I understand it. I never carried a revolver before in my life."

Feeny took the glistening, nickel-plated Smith & Wessen, clicked the hammer to the safety-notch, tested the cylinder springs, and, touching the lever, showed his superior by the feel rather than sight how the perfect mechanism was made to turn on its hinge and thrust the emptied shells from their chamber.

"The Lord grant we may have no call to shoot to-night, sir, but I misdoubt the whole situation. That fire's beginning to wear itself out already, and any minute I look to hear the hoof-beats of the Morales gang, surrounding us here on every side. If they'll only hold off till towards morning and I can brace up these two poor devils they've poisoned, we can stand 'em off a while until our fellows begin to come back or Lieutenant Drummond hears of the gathering."

"And do you still believe there are no Apaches in this business?" asked the major.

"Not out north or west, sir; they're thick enough ahead in the Santa Maria, but not to the north, not to the west; I can't believe that. Those Morales fellows know everything that is going on. They knew that just about this time Ned Harvey was expected along escorting his sisters home. They knew you had never seen him and could easily be made to believe the story. Everything has been done to hold us back, first at Ceralvo's and afterwards here, until they could gather all their gang in force sufficient to attack, then—Hist! listen! There's hoofs now. No, not out there, the other way, from the Tucson road, east. God grant it's some of our fellows coming back! Keep watch here, major; I'll run out and challenge."

Hastily picking up a carbine as he passed the door, Feeny ran nimbly out across the sandy barren, disappearing in the darkness to the southeast. Old Plummer's heart beat like a hammer as he listened for the hail. A moment more he could hear hoof-beats and the voices of men in low tones; then, low-toned too, but sharp and stern, Feeny's challenge rose upon the night:

"Who comes there?"

Instantly the invisible party halted, surprised; but with the promptness born of frontier experience, back came the answer:

"Friends."

"Who are you, and where from?"

"George Harvey and party from Tucson, looking for Moreno's. Who are you?"

"United States cavalry on escort duty. How many in your party?"

"Only two here. We were delayed by Apache signs in the Santa Maria. The rest are some miles behind with relay mules. Are we near the ranch? What's that light out to the west?"

"Never mind that now. Dismount and come up alone, Mr. Harvey; I must recognize you first."

Feeny wanted to gain time. His brain was whirling. Here was partial confirmation of the story told by the alleged Ned Harvey in the morning. Here was the father coming with guard and relay mules to meet his children just as their morning visitor declared he was expected to do. Was it possible after all that the tale was true,—that the children were there at the Gila, making wide *detour* around Ceralvo's and taking the northward route around that ill-favored ranch? If so, what awful tidings had he to break! Stout soldier that he was, Feeny felt that he was trembling from head to foot. Up through the gloom strode a tall figure, fearless and confident.

"There's no Irishman in all the Morales gang," laughed the coming man, "and I know a cavalryman's challenge when I hear it, and so honor it at once. Where are you, sentry?"

"Here; this way," answered Feeny, standing erect and

peering sharply through the gloom. "I've never met you, Mr. Harvey, but we all know you by reputation. Just tell me your business and how you happen to be riding the desert this time of night and then I'll tell you why I ask."

"I am expecting my son and daughters coming up from Yuma. We were to meet at Moreno's this evening; but a scouting-party in the mountains warned us to hide until night, so we're late. Have they reached Moreno's? We must be close there."

"You're close enough to Moreno's; it's not a hundred yards back there; but that light across the valley is the warning beacon at Picacho. They would hardly venture across knowing what that means."

"Why, my God, man!" exclaimed Harvey, "that says the Apaches are out west of the Santa Maria or the Christobal. Have you seen,—have you heard anything of them?"

"For the love of God, sir, don't ask me now. Come to the ranch. Major Plummer's there,—the paymaster. He'll tell you all we know."

A moment more and, with glaring eyes, with agonized, ashen face, the Arizona merchant stood at the entrance of the ranch, clinging to the horse-rail for support, listening with gasping breath to Plummer's faltering recital of the events of the morning.

"Are you sure it was my son,—my Ned?" he moaned.

"I never saw him before, Mr. Harvey; but some of my men were sure, and old Moreno here—"

The wooden shutter behind them swung open. From the

inner darkness Moreno's voice, tremulous with sympathy and distress, fell upon their ears.

"Senor Harvey, my heart bleeds for you. I saw him but an instant, but it was he,—Senor Edward, your son."

"God of heaven! and your men have gone, all of them?"

"All but Feeny here."

"Northeast, towards the Christobal?"

"Yes; but stop one moment now, and look at this note. Is it your son's writing?" And Plummer produced the crumpled page while Feeny held the light. Feverishly Harvey examined the scrawl, his hand trembling so hard he could not steady the paper.

"It is like enough," he moaned. "It was written in such mad haste. My horse!" he cried, "and you come with me, George. Send the others on our trail as soon as they get in. Give me another pistol if you can,—I have but one,—and in God's name order along the first troops that reach you."

Then in less than a minute even the galloping hoofs had muffled their dull thunder in the darkness and distance. With wild dread spurring him on, the father was gone to the rescue of his children, leaving old Plummer and his faithful sergeant shocked and nerveless at the ranch.

IV

And now, with such confirmation of the truth of the story of an Apache raid, the paymaster thought it only right to release Moreno from the duress in which Sergeant Feeny had placed him. When so old an inhabitant of Arizona as Mr. Harvey gave entire credence to the report; recognized the note as really his son's handiwork and hastened at all speed to overtake the pursuers, what room for doubt could be left in the mind of a new-comer to the soil? It was time, thought Plummer, to form an alliance, offensive and defensive, with the Mexican denizens of the ranch against the enemy common to both. But again Feeny shook his head in solemn protest.

"I may have been wrong as to the Apaches, sir, but I can't be mistaken as to Moreno. He's in the pay of the Morales brothers, even if not an active member of the gang. He is lurking in there now, I'll warrant you, with two or three of them in hiding, waiting for the coming of the main body. They'd 'a' been here before this, perhaps, if it hadn't been for the Apache story. They're more afraid of one of Cochises's band than of all the sheriffs from Tucson to Tacoma. I wish the rest of Harvey's people would get here," he continued, looking longingly out into the darkness. "Unless they are of better stuff than most of these mule-whackers in the Territory, you won't catch them hustling out alone trying to

Charles King

find their master this night. And yet, what use would they be to us?"

Plummer turned anxiously away and gave himself up to thought. Nothing but a faint glimmer now remained of the beacon-light. All was still as the grave about the lonely rancho. Walking over to the eastward door he entered the dark room, and was instantly hailed by the voice of his clerk.

"You're there, are you, Dawes?" he asked. "Not getting sleepy, I hope."

"Not a whit, major; I couldn't, even if I hadn't slept most of the day. I'm sitting here on the safe with a Colt's six-shooter in each hand. If old Moreno's door cracks, by gad! I'll let drive."

"Well, that's all right; but suppose they come around through the corral to this door?"

"I'm ready. I came within an ace of blazing away at you, but I happened to recognize your figure and step just in the nick of time."

A low whistle without broke up the colloquy. Plummer waddled off in the direction of the sound.

"What is it, sergeant?"

"They're coming, sir. Harvey's men, I mean. Will you deliver his message?"

"Just as you say; why shouldn't you?"

"It'll have so much more effect from your lips, major. They may misdoubt me."

Far out on the trail the quick-tripping hoofs of mules could now be heard. Presently a horseman shot up out of the gloom.

"Halt there!" sung out Feeny. "Whose party's this?"

"Harvey's, Tucson. Looking for Moreno's. Are we near?"

"You're there now, but you can't stop. Mr. Harvey wants you to come right along after him. He has taken the trail to the Christobal, where the Indians have carried off his daughters."

The man fairly reeled in saddle, shocked at the dreadful tidings.

"When?—how did it happen? Who's gone with him?"

"Some time this morning, from all we can learn. Two squads of cavalry are on the trail, one with Ned Harvey, the other just out from here at dark. The old man and George followed them as soon as they got in. Who's with you?"

"Two Mexicans, that's all; they're no account. I'd best leave them here with the mules. They're just behind and have been scared to death already."

And so in ten minutes two more of the low-caste, half-breed Mexicans were added to the paymaster's garrison, and Sergeant Feeny's brief exposition of the situation at the ranch only delayed the incoming American long enough to water his horse and stow a little grain in a sack.

"I wouldn't wonder a damned bit if the Morales gang *were* around here," was his discomforting assurance. "None of 'em have been seen about Tucson for a week before we left. Wish I could stay and stand by you, but my first duty is with

Mr. Harvey. I've been in his employ nigh on to eight years."

"What sort of looking man is Ned Harvey?" persisted the sergeant, still hopeful of some fraud.

"Tall, dark, smooth face; looks like a Spaniard almost. I never saw anybody who resembled him hereabouts. I'm afraid it's no plant. I don't want to offend you, sergeant, but I wish to God it *was* all the Morales gang's doings and that it was only your money they were after. If it's Apaches and they have got the old man's children, he'll never get over it."

"By heaven!" muttered Feeny to himself, as the loyal fellow put spurs to his horse and disappeared,—"by heaven! I begin to believe it's both."

And now with gloomy face the sergeant returned to where he had left Major Plummer watching the westward trail. A brief word at the door-way assured him the clerk was still alert and ready. A pause under the open window, high above the ground, of the room where slept Moreno's wife and daughter, if they slept at all, told him that all was silence there if not slumber, and then he joined his superior.

"That fellow was of the right sort, sergeant," said Plummer. "I wish we had one or two like him."

"I wish we had, sir; those Greasers are worse than no guards at all. They'll sit there in the corral and smoke *papellitos* by the hour, and brag about how they fought their way through the Apaches with Harvey's mules; but for our purpose they're worse than useless. At the first sign of an attack they'd be stampeding out into the darkness, and that's the last we'd see of them. Heard anything further out this way, sir?"

"Why, confound it! yes. I try to convince myself it's only

imagination; but two or three times, far out there towards the Picacho, I've heard that whip cracking. I have felt sure there was a hammering sound, as though some one were pounding on a wagon-tire. Once I was sure I heard a horse snort. *That* I was in a measure expecting. If those fellows mean to attack, they'll come mounted, of course; but what wagon would they have?"

"One of Ceralvo's, perhaps, to cart off the safe in, if they couldn't bust into it here."

"There! Hark now, sergeant! didn't you hear?" suddenly spoke the major, throwing up a warning hand.

Both men held their breath, listening intently. For a moment nothing but the beating of their own hearts served to give the faintest sound. Then, out to the west, under the starlit vault of the heavens, somewhere in that black expanse of desert, plainly and distinctly there rose the measured sound of iron or stone beating on iron. Whether it were tire or linch-pin, hame or brake, something metallic about a wagon or buckboard was being pounded into place or shape.

"It's them, sir," muttered the sergeant; "it's that bloody gang, for there's no stage due to-night, and if it was Harvey's ambulance, recaptured, 'tis from the northeast it would be coming."

"Mightn't they have missed the trail in the darkness, and, having no ranch lights to guide them, got lost somewhere out there?"

"Not likely, sir; shure there'd be a squad of the troop and half a dozen old hands with 'em if it was Harvey's. This has come from the pass, and it won't be long before they'll be coming ahead. You'll need your carbine then. Damn that man

Mullan! can't I wake him yet?"

Apparently not; even the well-directed kick only evoked a groan. Taking a couple of carbines, Feeny returned to the major, silently handing him one of the weapons, saying, "It's loaded, sir, and here's more cartridges."

Then again both men listened intently.

No sound now. The hammering had ceased. One—two minutes they waited, then nearer at hand than before, clear, sharp, and distinct, out from the darkness came the unmistakable crack of a whip. At the sound Feeny knelt. Click, click went the hammer of his carbine to full cock. Another moment of breathless silence. Then the muffled sound of hoofs, the creak of wagon-springs, then a voice,—

"It can't be far away. Ride ahead and see if you can't rout somebody out."

And then Feeny's challenge again rang out on the still night air, followed instantly by muffled sound of stir and excitement in the ranch behind them.

"Who comes there?"

"Hello! What's that? Who's that? Is that Moreno?"

"Who comes *there*, I say? Halt! or I'll fire."

"For God's sake don't fire, man; we've got ladies here."

"What ladies? Who are you anyhow? Quick!"

"George Harvey's daughters, of Tucson. I'm his son."

"God be praised!" shouted Feeny, springing to his feet and rushing forward. "Are they all safe?—unharmed? Where did you overtake them?"

"Overtake who? What in blazes are you talking about?" queried a tall, slender fellow, bending down from his saddle. "Who are you?"

"Sergeant Feeny, of the cavalry,—and here's the major just back of me."

"Major who?"

"Major Plummer; him you was talking with this morning when you came for help," answered Feeny, his voice tremulous with excitement. Already he was beginning to see light.

"Why, I've never seen Major Plummer nor any other major to-day. The only troops I met were Sergeant Wing and his guard at the pass just after nightfall. Have you met the Apaches? You saw the signal, of course."

"Signal, yes, but devil an Apache. Tell me now, wasn't it you was here at Moreno's this morning begging for troops to go and fetch your ladies down from the Gila? Wasn't it you sent the note saying they was run off by Indians?" And, as was the case whenever excited, Feeny's grammar ran to seed.

"Not a bit of it. My sisters are here, safe and sound. We'd have been here an hour ago but for slipping a tire. Is father here?"

"Talk to him, major; I'm done up entirely," was all poor Feeny could say, as, between relief, rejoicing, and the inestimable comfort of finding he was right in his theories after all, he dropped his carbine, threw himself upon the soft, sandy ground, and fairly rolled over and over in his excitement and emotion.

What wondering eyes,—what startled ears were at the wagon door-way, as, in his ponderous manner, the major endeavored to tell of the morning's adventure and the counterfeit presentment of the Ned Harvey now before him! Long before he could finish, the thoughtful son begged an instant's interruption.

"And father has gone on the trail to the Christobal?"

"Yes, an hour ago."

"After him, Leon! Ride like the devil, even if you have to ride all night. Fetch him back here as quick as you can. Tell him Fan and Ruth are safe here at Moreno's."

In ten minutes the Concord wagon with its fair freight, now trembling and excited, was standing side by side with the paymaster's ambulance. The weary mules were unhitched and, with the saddle-horses, led in to water. The major and the sergeant, prompting each other, went on with their recital, Harvey listening with attentive ear.

"It is one of the most perfect plants they ever put up," he burst in, grinding his teeth in wrath. "Of course they knew of father's movements and of mine. They know everything. They knew we were to meet here, probably. They felt assured you knew nothing of it at all. They have used our supposed peril to draw away your guard. They have succeeded even better than they planned, for they have drawn off father, too, and four of our best men into the bargain. But to think that this old scoundrel Moreno should be in it. We've always suspected the Ceralvo set; but father has done everything for Moreno,—practically built this ranch for him, dug his well, set him up in business, and now he makes this a rendezvous for thugs and assassins. By heaven! I'm glad you have him trapped. How many has he with him, do you think?"

"I don't know. I only feel sure he must have one or two, but it's the main gang we have to watch," answered Feeny; "they may be along any minute, and I thought it was them when we heard you."

"And that's what is worrying me, Mr. Harvey," said the major, as he drew the young man aside. "All they are after now, of course, is my safe full of money. It is my business to defend it to the last, and they can't have it without a fight. You and your sisters, ordinarily, they would not molest, but by this time they know you are here. Very possibly they've followed closely on your trail and may be gathering all around us at this moment. Let me be brief. The sooner you can hitch in those mules again, or those relay mules rather, and get out of here, the better."

"Ah! but, major, how about the Apaches in the Santa Maria? We would get there, you know, just about daybreak."

"By Jupiter! I never thought of them. You wouldn't have your guard now that your father's gone?"

"No. We've simply got to stay here, major. Personally, I'm only too glad to be here to help you out. It cannot be long before the troops come hurrying back when they find they've been tricked. Very probably they have found it out by this time." Then with quick decision he stepped back to the door of the Concord. "Girls! Paquita! Ruthie! tumble out, both of you; we're to stay here at Moreno's to-night." And, the paymaster aiding, the silent, trembling sisters were lifted from the wagon and led away into the one guest-room, the east room, where, pistol in hand, still sat Dawes on the safe. The wraps and pillows were quickly passed in. The little hurricane-lamp was stood in one corner. A bundle of cavalry blankets, left behind by the detachment when it took the trail, was spread out upon the earthen floor. The safe was hauled into the empty bar-room, and, bidding his sisters lie down and fear nothing, assuring them of their perfect safety there and urging them to sleep all they could against their move at dawn, Edward Harvey, looking well to his arms and bidding his two men do likewise, came forth and joined his soldier friends.

"There are five of us now against Morales and his outfit, and I'll just bet my horse we can thrash 'em."

"Only eleven o'clock," muttered old Plummer, as he struck a match and consulted his watch. "It's been the longest evening I ever spent; but, thank God, our worst fears are at an end. I never doubted for a moment that your sisters were captives. Who could the man have been who personated you?"

"I don't know. I've heard of him once before. He is about my height and build, but darker they say, and with more of Mexico in his manner. He has been to Tucson, but I never heard of his masquerading over my name until now, though I have heard of the resemblance. He must have copied my writing, too, to so completely fool father."

"Oh, that was a mere scrawl on soft paper with a broad-pointed pencil. There was no time to scrutinize it closely," explained the major. "Now, Feeny, you're officer of the guard. How do you want to post us?"

"It's what I've been thinking of, sir, ever since Mr. Harvey got in, and we've no time to lose. We can't loop-hole this adobe now, but we can barricade the door of these two rooms and stand off a good-sized gang. Mr. Harvey will, of course, want to be where he can look after the ladies; but if I can put one of his men in the corral, one who can be relied upon to shoot down any of Moreno's people who should try to come out, I think we can look out for the rest. Any minute now they'll be coming. First thing, run these two wagons around to the corral, so as to clear the approaches. There mustn't be anything behind which they can hide or take shelter." And, laying hold of the pole while willing hands manned the spokes, Feeny soon had the Concord and the weather-beaten ambulance safely out of the way. Then came a moment of consultation as to which of Harvey's men would be best suited for the onerous post opposite the enemy's door, and then a sudden and breathless silence.

"Listen!" whispered Feeny. "That's a signal. Hist! you'll hear it again presently."

Grasping their rifles with nervous hands, the five men stood huddling in a little group at the west end of the low, flat building.

Somewhere out on the dark expanse towards the peak a long, low whistle, ending in an abrupt high note, had sounded. For a moment there was no repetition. The invisible foe was signalling for reply. From whom could answer be expected but Moreno?

"Watch the old scoundrel's window there and this shutter over here," whispered the sergeant, indicating a board-covered port in the westward wall. "They'll try to show a light, perhaps. Run round into the corral and smash the first man that tries to come out. I'll tend to any feller that shows a head hereabouts."

Harvey turned with his employe and ran with him as far as the other end of the ranch. Here he entered the low doorway. The little lamp burned dimly, but two pairs of dark, dilated eyes gleamed eagerly upon him.

"I'm going to close this door now, girlies," he whispered. "Lie still. Do not venture near it or the window, and don't be frightened. It looks as though some of the Morales gang were around here hoping to find the paymaster unguarded. We'll give them a lesson they'll never forget, if they attempt to attack him."

For all answer Ruth Harvey only nestled closer to her sister and clung to her for courage and support. Paquita, however, became Amazonian at once.

"Is there nothing I can do, Ned? I can't bear to lie here listening and taking no part. Surely I could shoot a pistol well enough."

"You can help us best and most by lying flat and showing not so much as a finger at the door. We can tend to them, Fan. It won't be long before father and the troop come galloping back. Don't show a light now unless we call." Then he darted to the bar-room.

"Are they coming?" hailed the clerk, in a hoarse whisper.

"Somebody signalled out on the plain. It's probably they. Look out for Moreno now; don't let him or anybody through that door."

Far out on the desert again, louder, shriller, clearer, the whistle was repeated.

"Ah, blow and be damned to ye!" muttered Feeny. "There's

no answer from here ye'll get this night. Watch out now. Some of 'em will try to crawl up after a little."

But nearly five minutes passed without other sign or sound. Then, closer in, a horse stamped and snorted; a coarse Mexican voice muttered a savage oath. Feeny, crouching low, darted into the darkness in the direction of the sound. Plummer and Harvey would have restrained him, but it was too late; he was gone before either could speak. Then a latch creaked and snapped behind them and, slowly and cautiously, the wooden shutter began to open outward. In an instant Harvey had raised his rifle and struck the resounding board a fierce blow with the butt. The door flew back, crashing in violent contact against the grizzled pate of Moreno himself, who, with a howl of mingled rage and anguish, fell back from the aperture.

"Open that again and I'll blow your head off, you scoundrel!" growled Harvey. "Don't you dare show hair nor hide outside your room. Every man has orders to shoot you on sight, if that's any comfort to you."

Only for a second had the old Mexican's head appeared; only an instant had he for plea or protestation, but that instant had served to show a narrow streak of light from the room within, and this mere crack revealed to the watchful eyes out upon the plain the position of the ranch, possibly told them something more, for in less than half a minute two horsemen came looming up out of the darkness and cantering fearlessly towards them. Phlegmatic as he was, old Plummer's nerves gave a twitch as, sharp and stern, young Harvey challenged.

"Halt there! Who are you? *Halt*! or we fire."

"Friends," shouted one voice; "Americans," the other, as promptly the order to halt was obeyed, the trained horses going almost on their haunches under the cruel force of the huge Mexican bit.

"We are seeking Moreno's," continued the first voice. "The Apaches jumped our outfit just after sunset and we had to run for it."

"How many are there of you all told?" demanded Harvey.

"Only us two. We're partners, prospecting,—been down towards the Sonora line. For the Lord's sake, gentlemen, don't keep us out here. We've lost everything we had,— packs, packers, and grub. We're about dead beat for a drink and something to eat."

"What do you think of this, major?" whispered Harvey. "Those are Americans sure."

"Well, I'd let'em in," said the major; "but where the devil's Feeny? He's the best judge, really. Their story may be all true. They may be alone."

"I don't know; it isn't likely. You heard that voice out there a moment ago; that was Mexican beyond any doubt. We've got to stand those fellows off till we hear from Feeny." Then, raising his voice, Harvey called,—

"Just stay where you are a moment. You're all right perhaps, but our guards have orders to be on the lookout for Morales and his gang, and you might get shot by mistake."

"Well, for God's sake turn out your men, if you've got any, and help us catch these murdering thieves," was the impatient reply. "How many are you?"

"Oh, there's plenty of us here," was Harvey's cheery answer.

"Most of 'C' troop; but we've other business on hand just now. You wait there quietly for a minute or two until the sergeant comes around with the patrol; he'll see to you."

And then, as though the whole thing had been planned beforehand, out in the darkness to the north Feeny's voice was heard in low-toned but sharp command,—

"Patrol, halt! Close up there, Kennedy. Where are you, Number Five?" And so, cool and confident as though he had a dozen troopers at his back, Feeny came striding up to the spot.

"What's the matter, sentry? Didn't I hear you parleying here with somebody?"

"Two strangers out there, sergeant;—say they're prospectors and been jumped by Apaches."

"Hwere away are they?" Then in low tone, "Go you out beyond the corral," he whispered to old Plummer. "There's four of them out there. Challenge if they try to come in." Then aloud again, "Shure, I don't see anything, sentry."

"Right out ahead there, sergeant. Two men, mounted."

"Come down, one of ye. Dismount and come in here. Lave your gun behind. Give your reins to your pal there," was Feeny's next mandate.

There was a moment of hesitation, a faint sound of whispering as though the self-styled prospectors were in consultation, and again Feeny spoke in tone more sharp and imperative,—

"Dismount one, I say. Come in here, or I'll send a bullet for your cards. Quick now."

Charles King

Still another delay. The "prospectors" seemed anxious to edge off into deeper darkness.

"If ye're not off that horse's back in ten seconds, be jabers, I'll fire, so be lively." And as his excitement rose so did Feeny's Irish.

Four—five seconds ticked by and still there was no approach. Fiercely, with sharp emphasis, the sergeant brought his carbine to full cock. "It's aiming I am," said he, as he quickly raised the butt to his shoulder. There was a sudden scurry and scramble of horses' hoofs, low-voiced words of warning and a muttered curse or two. Then leaped a tongue of fire into the night, and from the corral corner came sharp report, followed by a cry, a gurgle, a groan, then silence.

"My God! they've shot the major," exclaimed Harvey, as he leaped away in the direction of the shot. At the same moment away sped the two horsemen in front of the post. No use to fire. They were shrouded in thick darkness and out of harm's way before one could pull trigger. Then came two flashes, two quick reports, then half a dozen rapid, sputtering revolver-shots, then a vengeful howl and a rush out on the plain. Feeny ran like a deer on the trail of Mr. Harvey, and in less time than it takes to tell it they came upon the paymaster, sinking shocked and nerveless to the sandy soil, his hands clasping on his side.

"Pick him up, you and your man there; carry him into the ranch. I'll bate back those blackguards yet," muttered Feeny, as he took a quick snap shot at some dim object flitting across the plain and sent another into the darkness, aiming vaguely where he could hear the thud of horses' hoofs. For a moment, running from point to point after each discharge, he kept up a rapid fusillade, under cover of which the hapless paymaster was borne swiftly away around the corner of the ranch and carried into the bar, where, wild with anxiety, but faithful to his trust, Mr. Dawes still guarded the safe. Then Harvey stepped through the narrow door-way to the eastern room.

"I have to borrow the lamp a moment, Fan," he whispered. "Now lie still. We may have to stand a siege awhile until father can reach us."

Two minutes more, bending low and with his last cartridge crammed into the chamber of his carbine, Feeny turned to make a run for the ranch. Just as he came speeding in past the westward wall the wooden shutter was hurled open and a strange voice, loud, exultant, strident, burst upon his ear.

"Come on, Pasqual! Come—"

But the rest was lost in the roar of Feeny's ready weapon. The rude facade of adobe blazed red one instant in the flash of the carbine and the loud report went bellowing out across the plain. But within the ranch there went up a wail of terror and dismay, for Ramon Morales, shot through the brain, was stretched lifeless at the feet of Moreno and his shuddering wife.

And then Feeny, unscathed, leaped inside the bar-room.

"Now for it, men! Drag in those two drunken brute bastes," he cried, laying hold of Mullan's limp carcass. "Lug in wan of them water-jars. Stick their damned heads into that trough beyant. Now be lively. The whole gang'll be on us in less than a minute."

V

At midnight the situation at Moreno's ranch was a strange one. The occupants of the two rooms farthest to the east were being besieged by ten or fifteen outlawed men, some Mexican, some "Gringo," but all cut-throats, and up to this moment the besieged had had the best of it.

And yet their plight was desperate. In the easternmost room, secure from bullet or missile of any kind so long as they crouched close to the ground and back from the door-way, lay trembling in silence old Harvey's daughters. At the door, only the barrel of his rifle protruding, keeping under cover all he possibly could behind an improvised parapet of barley-bags, knelt their devoted brother, cool and determined, every now and then whispering words of hope and encouragement. In the adjoining room, connected with the eastern chamber by a doorless aperture through the adobe wall, lay the paymaster, sorely wounded, but still conscious and plucky, his faithful clerk ministering to him as best he could, stanching the flow of blood and comforting him with cool water. At the door-way opening on the hard-trampled space at the southern front of the ranch, sheltering himself behind his breastwork of barley, but never relaxing vigilant watch, knelt Sergeant Feeny, a bandana bound about his forehead, the blood trickling down his right cheek, the sleeve of his flannel shirt rent by a bullet that just grazed the upper arm.

Kneeling on the counter and peeping through a hole in the bottom of the wooden window-shutter, one of Harvey's men kept guard, the other faced the door-way into Moreno's domestic apartments, every now and then letting drive a shot through the wood-work to keep them, as he said, "from monkeying with the bolt on the other side." In planning his roadside ranch Moreno had allowed outer doors only to those rooms which were for public use; the three which lay to the west of the bar could not be entered except through that resort or by a door giving on the corral, both of these doors being supplied with massive bolts as security against intruders, and all three rooms being furnished with air-ports rather than windows, pierced at such a height through the adobe that no one from without, except in saddle, could peer through the aperture and see what was going on within. The travellers' room and the bar-room ports, however, were low and large, and all the rooms were spacious; the bar, of course, being the dining as well as drinking-room, carried off the honors in point of size. This, too, was furnished with an opening into the corral, but Feeny's, first thought on reaching his comrades was to barricade. Springing into the walled enclosure and bidding Harvey watch while the others worked, he had soon succeeded in lugging a score of big barley-sacks into the interior and piling them into breast-works at the three doors, the one opening into the corral being provided in addition with a high "traverse" to protect its guard against shots that might come through from Moreno's room. All this was accomplished amidst the wailing of the Mexican women and the fusillade begun by the assailants in hopes of terrorizing the defence before venturing to closer quarters. Like famous Croghan, of Fort Stephenson, Feeny had kept up a fire from so many different points as to impress the enemy with the idea there were a dozen men and a dozen guns where there was in reality only one, and even the temptation of that vast sum in the paymaster's safe was not sufficient to nerve the followers of

Morales to instant attack. The valor and vigor of the defence and the appalling death of one of their leaders had so unnerved them that Pasqual himself, raging, imploring, threatening by turns, was unable to urge them to close quarters. "Most men are cowards in the dark" is a theory widely believed in. Indians certainly are only brave against defenceless women and children at such a time. Not until the firing had ceased and it was evident that the defenders had retired to the shelter of the ranch, and then only very slowly and cautiously, would these brigands of the desert be induced to resume their stealthy approach. For full half an hour there was a lull in the fight, and then, guided by the light Moreno was now able to show, Pasqual and two of the stouter-hearted knaves approached the western wall and held brief consultation with the rascally owner. Rage at the death of their leader's brother and ally, the thirst for vengeance, and the hope of securing such rich booty, all were augmented by Moreno's fiery assurances and encouragement. All the soldiers were gone, he said, except the "pig of a sergeant" and two drugged and senseless swine. Somebody among them was wounded. There were only three, possibly four, left. Let his *companeros* make combined attack, two or three through his (Moreno's) rooms, two or three rush in from the corral, and the same number from the south front at once, and beyond doubt the cursed Yankees would succumb. Then, no quarter, no quarter for the men. His connection with the outlaw band was now known and these witnesses must be put to death. Then—then the paymaster's safe could readily be battered open, then there was the mint of money to be divided among the victors, then away to Sonora with their spoil and with old Harvey's beautiful daughters. What ransom would he not be willing to pay,—that proud, disdainful father! Was ever luck so great? But haste! haste!—not a moment could be lost; they must act at once.

And so Morales hurried to station and instruct his men.

Prowling like coyotes through the darkness and at respectful distance from the guarded end of the ranch, half a dozen of the number crept into the corral. Others were distributed over the southern front. Three of the lighter and more slender of the band were "boosted" through the high west window into Moreno's domain. Then through the middle room they made their way, where sat the senora, rocking, weeping, and moaning over the body of the outlaw leader, where, hiding under the bed, shivering and praying, crouched the senorita, her daughter, and then, barefooted, they crept into the room adjoining the bar and listened, breathless, to the low-toned instructions of the veteran sergeant. From without no glimmer of light could guide the assailants or help them in their aim. The black apertures of the door-ways were poor marks for night shooting, and the more enterprising and adventurous, crawling like snakes to reconnoitre, were soon able to report that most scientifically had the defence thrown up their breastworks. From group to group flitted Pasqual. At his shrill battle-cry all hands were to rush simultaneously to the attack, firing no shot for fear of hitting one another; but with pistol in one hand and the long, deadly knife in the other, close at once upon the defenders, leap over their barriers and overwhelm them in the dark interior. In three minutes the signal would be given. He himself would lead the dash of the party within the corral. Pasqual was shrewd enough to know that where there was only one door-way instead of two there would be better chance of dodging the bullets. But keen eyes and ears and wits were there alert. Feeny and Harvey well knew that this was but the lull before the storm.

"Lay low, boys, and be ready. Shoot the first man that shows," was the last caution old Plummer heard before the bursting of the tempest.

All on a sudden a wild cry went up in the corral. All on a

sudden from north and south the assailants dashed forward with answering yell. In an instant the dark apertures flashed their lightning, and rifle and revolver-shots rang on the still night air. Harvey's Henry barked like a Gatling; Feeny's old Springfield banged like a six-pounder. Two of the assailants on the south side went down in the dust, face foremost, the others swerved, broke, and scurried for shelter. Pasqual Morales, leading his men close under the north wall, made a panther-like spring for the crest of the barley parapet, and was saved from instant death when he fell by being dragged feet foremost, with a Colt's forty-four tearing through his thigh. In vain Moreno's squad fired shot after shot through the wooden door; their bullets buried themselves deep in the improvised traverse but let no drop of blood, while two return shots scattered the attack with the splinters from the heavy panels. Pleading, raging, maddened, Morales learned that the dash had failed, and that two of his most daring men, the two Americanos who had ridden forward to personate prospectors and who had led the rush in the southern front, were knocked out of the fight.

And then it was that the inhuman brute gave the order to resort to Indian methods, and even old Moreno begged and prayed and blasphemed all to no purpose. Furious at their repulse, the band were ready to obey their leader's maddest wish. The word was "Burn them out." Ned Harvey, crouching behind his barley-bags, felt his blood turn to ice water in his veins when, with exultant yells and taunts, the corral suddenly lighted up with a broad red glare. The match had been applied to the big hay-stack close to the brush-covered shed, close to the "leanto" under which so much inflammable rubbish was stored. It could be a question of only a few moments, then they, too, would be a mass of flames spreading rapidly westward. The stout adobe wall separating the ranch proper from the sheds would protect the occupants from direct contact with the flame, but what could save the roof? Stretching from wall to wall were the dry, resinous pine logs that formed the basis of the bulky structure; over these the lighter boards of pine; and over all, thickly piled, dry as bone and inflammable as tinder, heap on heap of brush. Once this was fairly ablaze the hapless occupants of the rooms beneath might as well be under the grating of some huge furnace.

High in air shot the leaping flames. Far and wide over the desert spread the lurid glare. Screaming with terror, the women of Moreno's household were already dragging into the corral their few treasures and rushing back for such raiment as they could save. Far over at the corral gate, where the bullets of the besieged could not find them, Pasqual Morales and his exulting band were gathered, the chief lying upon his *serape* with bloody bandages about his leg, his followers dancing about him in frantic glee, all keeping carefully out of range of the black door-ways, yet three or four crack shots lay flat in the sands, their rifles covering the now glaring fronts of the threatened rancho, ready to shoot down, Indian-like, the wretched garrison when driven out.

It was at this juncture that from somewhere in the middle room behind Moreno's heavy door a voice was heard.

"Hand out the safe. Hand out your money now and we'll leave you in peace. Every man of us will ride away, and you can come out as soon as we are gone. Answer, for you have no time to lose."

"Answer him, you!" shouted Feeny to Mr. Dawes. "Send a shot through and hit him if you can."

But before the clerk could drop the fan with which he was striving to revive his fainting chief, the young fellow from Harvey's party, he who was stationed at the north door and had been so fortunate as to shoot Morales himself, now suddenly sprang from his covert and, placing the muzzle of his Henry rifle close to the door, deliberately popped three shots in quick succession through the splintering wood-work, and, in the confusion and dismay which resulted, was able to leap nimbly into his corner again before the answering shots could come.

"Take that for your answer," shouted Feeny again, "you black-hearted, black-bellied thafe, and take this, too, bad scran to ye! Every dollar of that money's in greenbacks that'll burn as aisy as tissue, and if you want it, come and get it now. 'Tis you that's got no time to lose. Come and get it, I say, for be the soul of St. Patrick you'll never have another chance. Just as sure as ye let that fire reach this ranch and harm those young leddies,—old Harvey's daughters that never did ye a harm in the world,—every dollar in the safe goes whack into the fire, and sorra a shinplaster will you have for all your pains. Ain't that so, paymasther? Shure the government ought to be mighty glad of the chance of saving all those promises to pay."

"Bravo, Feeny!" shouted young Harvey from the adjoining room. "We're not smoked out yet by a good deal," he added in lower tone. "But if the worst comes to the worst we can make a rush for the barley-stack in the corral. Lie still, Ruth, little sister; it won't be any time now before the soldiers will come galloping to us." And, hiding her terror-stricken face in her sister's breast, the girl obeyed.

Out at the corral gate meantime a vehement council was being held. Feeny's bold defiance and threat had produced their effect. His voice had rung out above the roar of the flames, and what Morales could not hear was promptly reported by those who had crawled up nearer to the bar and could understand every word. Even hampered by the care of their helpless women, the defence was undismayed; the little garrison was fighting with magnificent hope and courage. Beyond the wounding of one of their number, no impression apparently had been made, whereas the bandits had a sorry loss to contemplate. Ramon shot dead, Pasqual crippled, and the two "Gringos," the daring and enterprising leaders of the attack, painfully wounded, one probably mortally so. And now with the flames lighting up the whole valley between the Picacho and the Christobal, with cavalry known to be out in several squads within easy march, some of the men were already weakening. They had had enough of it and were quite ready to slink away; but Pasqual was a raging lion. Revenge for the death of his brother, wrath over his own crippled condition, fury at the failure of the assault, and hatred on general principles of all honest means and honest men, all prompted him to order and enforce a renewal of the attack, all served to madden him to such a degree that even burning his adversaries to death seemed simply a case of serving them right. What cared he that two of the besieged were fair young girls, non-combatants? They were George Harvey's daughters, and that in itself was enough to bring balm to his soul and well-nigh cause him to forget his physical ills. One or two of the band strove to point out that the faintest indignity offered to the sisters would array not only all Arizona, but all Mexico against them. Like dogs they would be hunted to their holes and no quarter be given. Returning hitherto with their spoils, Chihuahua or Sonora had welcomed them with open arms; but what outlaw could find refuge in Mexican soil who had dared to wrong the children of George Harvey and Inez Romero? It was even as they were pointing this out to Pasqual and urging that he consent to be lifted into the ambulance and driven away southward before the return of the cavalry, that Moreno himself appeared. Slipping out of his western window, dropping to the ground and making complete circuit of the corral, he suddenly joined in the excited conference. What he said was in Spanish, or that pan-Arizona *patois* that there passes current for such, and was a wild, fervid appeal. They had ruined him, him and his. He was unmasked, betrayed, for now his connection with the band was established beyond all question; now he was known and would soon be branded as an outlaw. His home was being destroyed before his eyes,—not that that amounted to much now that he could no longer occupy it,—his wife and child must flee at once for Sonora and he go with them, but recompense for his loss he must have; never again could he venture into Arizona: he would be known far and wide as the betrayer of his benefactor's children, though he called God and all the saints in the Spanish calendar to witness he never dreamed of their being involved in his plot. The paymaster's funds, not the lives of any of the paymaster's men, were what he had sought to take, and now, there lay the dollars almost within their grasp, but unless captured at once would be gone forever.

"I know that pig of a sergeant,—may the flames of hell envelop him for all eternity!" he cried. "He will not scruple to do as he says. He will cast every package into the seething furnace. *Mira!* Look; the shed is now all ablaze. In one minute the roof of the rancho will burst into flame. There is not an instant to lose. I adjure you let the daughters of Harvey, the son, the men come out at once; swear to them safety, honor, protection. Let them go their way now, now. Then you will have to deal with only two or three, and the treasure is ours. Look you, Sanchez, Pedro, Jose, down with that shed next the rancho! hurl it, drag it down so that its fire cannot reach the brush beyond, then we can parley, we can win their ear. They will be but too glad to be spared to go on their way unharmed. Yonder are their mules across the corral. Hitch them in at once. Save the others for the ambulance and the buck-board here, and for our noble chief. Is it not so, capitan? Am I not right?"

Approving murmurs followed his fiery words. So long as the Yankees held together there was little likelihood of the outlaws gaining the ground except by burning out, and that now meant the destruction of the very money they were after, the utter loss of the fortune that, divided even among so many, would enable them to live like princes in Hermosillo or beyond. They would be heroes, conquerors. But if that were lost after all their plotting, planning, labor, and crime, there was absolutely no recompense. Even through the brain-clouding fury of his revenge Pasqual Morales saw the sound sense of Moreno's plea. He made no effort to check the men who ran to do his bidding and were even now with lariats and stalwart arms dragging the props from under the shed and letting its western end come pattering down. Within the eastern room the dense smoke was already finding its way. The sound of falling beams and timber only conveyed to the occupants the idea that already the shed was in embers, and that any instant the roof over their heads would burst into a torrent of fire. Ned Harvey's brave spirit was taxed to the utmost. Unless relief could come and come at once, nothing remained for him but death, nothing for those fair sisters but a fate far worse.

At one instant he was on the point of urging the paymaster to comply with the outlaws' demand, pledging himself and his father's fortune to make good to the government every cent so sacrificed. His father could pay it four times over, and would rather sink his last cent than that the faintest harm should come to those beloved children; but the next moment Feeny's splendid defiance had so thrilled him that he could not frame the words he thought to speak, and yet, here was awful peril close at hand. What right had he to further jeopard the life, the honor, of these, his father's fondest treasures? If it were only himself it would be stay and fight it out to the bitter end. But if the robbers could now be content with the money alone and pledge safeguard for the party, was it not his duty, would it not be his father's mandate were he there, to buy the safe and contents from the agent of the general government and pay the ransom levied?

But he little dreamed of the fury of revenge and hatred burning in the soul of Pasqual Morales. He little fathomed the treachery and cunning of the outlawed scoundrel. Even as he was revolving these thoughts in mind, ever and again listening with new hope for the sound of rallying trumpet, the beat of rescuing hoofs, there resounded through the night the sonorous and ringing voice that so short a time before had called for the surrender of the safe.

"Edward Harvey, we pledge safe-conduct for you, your sisters, and your party. Here is your wagon ready, your team hitched in. Throw your arms out of the door. Come forth as you please. Put the senoritas in the wagon. Look neither to the right nor left, but drive away, and God be with you. We have no quarrel with you and yours. We war only with these soldiers who have killed our chief."

Put yourself in his place. Death for him, perhaps for them,— dishonor anyway,—was all they could look for if no rescue came. Was it not his duty to his parents, to his sisters, even to God, to accept these terms,—to withdraw his little force? Why should he be perilling such precious lives and names in the defence of a government official who had been so reckless as to part with his guard and put himself and his funds in such a predicament? From the other room in which the major now lay, feebly moaning, no word of remonstrance came. Even in their extremity, then, the soldiers of the government would not urge that he stay and encounter further peril in their defence. One of the drugged troopers was beginning to regain some atom of sense, and, sitting up, was miserably asking what had happened, what was the matter now.

"Go and douse water over your damned worthless head, Mullan," he heard the sergeant say, so Feeny was evidently alert as ever and must have heard the proposition from without. At his feet, huddled close to the floor where the thick smoke was least distressing, Fanny and Ruth still clung to one another, the latter trembling at the sound of the voice from without. But Fanny had quickly, eagerly, raised her head to listen. For a moment no reply was made. Then came the impatient query,—

"Harvey, do you hear? You have no time to lose. You have but a minute in which to answer."

"Major," he burst forth at last in an agony of doubt, "you hear what they say, you see how I am fixed. If I were here alone you would never need to ask my services, I'd fight with you to the bitter end; but think of my father,—my mother if anything befall my sisters. Can nothing be done?"

From the lips of the stricken paymaster there came only a groan in reply.

"I fear he cannot hold out long, Mr. Harvey," muttered the clerk. "I doubt if he heard or understood you."

"Well, why not let them have the safe if they'll guarantee that that is all they want? How much have you there? I feel sure my father would make it good."

"There's over twenty-five thousand dollars, Mr. Harvey."

"Well, if it was only twenty-five cents, Mr. Ned Harvey, all I've got to say is, devil a wan of them would they get so long as I could load a shot or pull a trigger. Go you if you will; take the leddies by all means if you think it safer; but before I'd trust the wan sister I ever had—God rest her soul—to the promise of any such blackguard party as this, I'd bury my knife in her throat."

An awful stillness followed Feeny's words. For an instant there was no sound but quick-beating hearts, the mutterings and complainings of poor Mullan, staggering about in search of his carbine, the quickened breath and low moaning of poor old Plummer. Then again came the loud hail from without.

"Once more, Ned Harvey, will you come out and be saved, or stay there and roast? Surrender now and you're all right; but, by the God of heaven, if you refuse, it's the last chance for you or those you were fool enough to bring here. Think for your sisters, man. There's no hope for one of you if you delay another minute."

And then it was a woman's voice, tremulous but clear.

"Ned, wasn't it to save us that Major Plummer sent his men? Wasn't it for our sake he gave up all his escort?"

"It was, Fan, yes; at least he thought so."

"And now you would desert him, would you?—leave him to be murdered by these robbers, the worst gang we ever had or heard of. I say you shall not. I for one will not go into their hands. Ruth cannot go without me. Stay and fight it out, Ned, or you're not your father's son."

"Fan! Fan! you're a trump! God bless your brave heart!" cried Harvey. "It seemed cowardly to go, yet the responsibility was more than I could bear."

"May the saints in heaven smile on your purtty face for all eternity!" muttered Feeny, in a rapture of delight. "The young leddy is right, Mr. Harvey; though it wasn't for me to say it. Shure you can't trust those scoundrels; they'd stab ye in the back, sir, and rob you of your pretty sisters and drag them away before your dying eyes. That man Pasqual is a devil, sir, nothing less. Shure we'll fight till rescue comes, for come it will. I tell you the boys are spurring towards us, hell to split, from every side now, and we'll whale these scoundrels yet."

Then from without came the final hail,—

"What answer, Harvey? Now or never."

"Go to hell, you son of an ape and worse than a Greaser!" yelled Feeny. "If you had a dhrop of Irish blood in your veins ye'd never ask the question. Now if you think you can take this money, here's your chance. No Harvey ever went back on his friends."

Even brain-muddled Mullan felt a maudlin impulse to cheer at Feeny's enthusiastic answer. Even poor old Plummer gave a half-stifled cry. Possibly he dreamed that rescue was at hand; but there was little time for rejoicing. Springing back whence he came, the unseen emissary was heard shouting some order to his fellows. The next instant the rifles began their cracking on both sides, and the bullets with furious spat drove deep into the adobe or whizzed through the gunny-sacks into the barley. The unseen foe was once more investing them on every side and not a shot could be wasted in return. Once more the furious crackle and roar of flames was heard close at hand, and then the smoke grew thicker, the heat increased, and poor Ned Harvey, his eyes smarting, knelt steadfast at his post and prayed, prayed for the coming of rescue, for the return of the loved father, all the gallant troop at his back, and then—even as though in answer to his prayer—there came a sudden lull in the fight.

"Something's coming!" shouted Feeny, excitedly. "They see or hear somebody, sure. Look, Mr. Harvey, ain't that two of their fellows scudding away westward out there?"

Surely enough. In the glare of the burning sheds the besieged caught a glimpse of two of the gang bending low in their saddles a hundred yards away and scudding like hounds over towards the open plain.

"Is it rescue? Are our people coming?" was the query that rose to every lip. "God grant it!"

Heavens, how hearts were beating! How ears were straining underneath that now blazing roof! Louder, fiercer soared the flames; furious became the snapping of sun-baked branch and twig; stifling and thick the smoke.

"Quick! Come here for a breath of air," called Harvey to his sisters. "It's safe for a moment, at least." And instantly they joined him at the door-way, still clinging close to the floor.

Listen! Hoofs! The thunder of galloping steeds! A distant cheer! A soldierly voice in hoarse command,—

"Steady, steady there! Keep together, men!"

"God be praised!" screamed Feeny, in ecstasy. "Look up, major; look up, sir. We're all safe now. Here come the boys. Hurroo!" And mad with relief and delight, the sergeant sprang from his lair just as a tall trooper in the Union blue shot into sight in the full glare of the flames, sprang from his foaming steed, waving his hat and yelling,—

"All right! All safe, lads! Here we are!"

Down went Harvey's rifle as he leaped out into the blessed

air to greet the coming host. Down went Feeny's carbine as, with outstretched hand, he sprang to grasp his comrade trooper's. With rush and thunder of hoofs a band of horsemen came tearing up to the spot just as Feeny reached their leader,—reached him and went down to earth, stunned, senseless from a crashing blow, even as Ned Harvey, his legs jerked from under him by the sudden clip of rawhide lariat, was dragged at racing speed out over the plain, bumping over stick and stone, tearing through cactus, screaming with rage and pain, until finally battered into oblivion, the last sound that fell upon his ear was the shriek of agony from his sisters' lips, telling him they were struggling in the rude grasp of reckless and infuriated men.

VI

Harvey could not long have lain unconscious. No bones were broken, no severe concussion sustained in the rapid drag over the sandy surface, and the awful sense of the calamity that had befallen him and the dread and doubt as to the fate of his beloved ones seemed to rally his stunned and bewildered faculties and bring him face to face with the horror of the situation. Barely able to breathe, he found himself rudely gagged. Striving to raise his hand to tear the hateful bandage away, he found that he was pinioned by the elbows and bound hand and foot by the very *riata*, probably, that had dragged him thither. No doubt as to the nationality of his unseen captors here. The skill with which he had been looped, tripped, whisked away, and bound,—the sharp, biting edges, even the odor of dirty rawhide rope,—all told him that though Americans were not lacking in the gang, his immediate antagonists hailed from across the Sonora line. Who and what they were mattered little, however. The fact that after hours of repulse in open attack, the foe had all on a sudden carried their castle by a damnable ruse was only too forcibly apparent. Writhing, struggling in miserable effort to free himself from his bonds, poor Harvey's burning eyes were maddened by the picture before him only a couple of hundred yards away. There in the fierce light of the flames now bursting from every window and roaring and shooting high in air from the brush-heaped roof of Moreno's ranch,—

there stood the Concord wagon, stalwart men clinging to the heads of the plunging and excited mules, a big ruffian already in the driver's seat, whip and reins in hand; there beside it was the paymaster's ambulance, into which three of the gang were just shoving the green-painted iron safe,—the Pandora's box that had caused all their sorrows; there Moreno's California buck-board, pressed into service and being used to carry the wounded, drawn by the extra mules; and then—God of heaven! what a sight for brother's eyes to see and make no sign!—then one big brute lifted from the ground and handed up to a fellow already ensconced within the covered wagon the senseless, perhaps lifeless, form of pretty little Ruth, his father's idol. The poor child lay unresisting in the ruffian's arms, but not so Paquita. It took two men, strong and burly, to lift and force her into the dark interior, and one of those, to the uttermost detail of his equipment, was to all appearance a trooper of the United States cavalry. There stood his panting horse with hanging head and jaded withers, the very steed whose rush they had welcomed with such exceeding joy, saddled, bridled, blanketed, saddle-bagged, lariated, side-lined, every item complete and exactly as issued by the Ordnance Department. The trooper himself wore the field uniform of the cavalry,— the dark-blue blouse, crossed by the black carbine sling, whose big brass buckle Ned could even now see gleaming between the broad shoulders, and gathered at the waist by the old-fashioned "thimble belt" the troop saddlers used to make for field service before the woven girdle was devised. Even more: Harvey in his misery remembered the thrill of joy with which he had noted, as the splendid rider reined in and threw himself from the saddle, the crossed sabres, the troop letter "C," and the regimental number gleaming at the front of his campaign hat. Who—who could this be, wearing the honorable garb of a soldier of United States, yet figuring as a ringleader in a band of robbers and assassins now adding rapine to their calendar of crime? Edward Harvey's heart

Charles King

almost burst with helpless rage and wretchedness when he saw his precious sisters dragged within the canvas shelter,— saw the tall, uniformed brigand leap lightly after them, and heard him shout to the ready driver, "Now, off with you!"

Crack! went the whip as the men sprang from the heads of the frantic mules, and with a bound that nearly wrenched the trace-hooks from the stout whippletree, the Concord went spinning over the sands to the south, whirling so near him that over the thud of hoofs and whirl of wheels and creak of spring and wood-work he could hear poor Fanny's despairing cry,—the last sound he was aware of for hours, for now in dead earnest Harvey swooned away.

Half an hour later, the rafters of the ranch having by this time tumbled in and turned the interior into a glowing furnace, there came riding from the west a slender skirmish line of horsemen in the worn campaign dress of the regular cavalry. With the advance there were not more than six or eight, a tall, slender lieutenant leading them on and signalling his instructions. With carbines advanced, with eyes peering out from under the jagged hat-brims, the veteran troopers came loping into the light of the flames, expectant every instant of hearing the crack of outlaw's rifle, or perhaps the hiss of feathered arrow of unseen foe. Though some of the steeds looked hot and wearied, the big raw-boned sorrel that carried the young commander tugged at his bit and bounded impatiently as though eager for the signal—"charge." Straight into the circle of light, straight to the southern entrance, now a gate of flame, the soldier rode and loudly hailed "Moreno!"

But hissing, snapping wood-work alone replied. Guided by an experienced sergeant, some of the troopers, never halting, rode on into the eastward darkness, and there were stationed as videttes to guard against surprise. Returning to where he had passed his lieutenant, the sergeant dismounted, allowing

his weary horse to stand, and then began minute exami-
nation. Following the freshest hoof-tracks, he found the
young officer riding about through the thick smoke within
the corral.

"Any sign of Moreno or his people, sir?" he hailed.

"Not yet. Just see what's beyond that door-way. My horse is
frightened at something there and I can't see for the smoke."

Obedient, the sergeant pushed ahead, bending low to avoid
the stifling fumes. Between the tumbled-down heap of
barley-sacks and the crumbling wall lay some writhing
objects in the sand, and his stout heart almost failed him at
the moan of agony that met his ear.

"Help! water! Oh, for Christ's sake, water!"

One bound carried him out of sight of his superior. The next
instant, dragging by the foot a prostrate form, he emerged
from the bank into the fresher air of the centre of the corral.
Off came his canteen and was held to the parched lips of a
stranger in scorched civilian dress, his beard and hair singed
by the flames, his legs and arms securely bound.

"Who are you and what's happened? Whose work is this?"
demanded the lieutenant, leaping from saddle to his side. The
man seemed swooning away, but the sergeant dashed water
in his face.

"Quick!—the others!—or they'll burn to death."

"What others? Where, man?" exclaimed the soldiers,
springing to their feet.

"Oh! somewhere in there,—the far end of the corral—or

Moreno's west room," was the gasping reply.

Another rush into the whirling, eddying smoke, another search along under the wall, and presently in the flickering light the rescuing pair came upon a barrier of barley-sacks, burning in places from huge flakes of fire falling from the blazing rafters of the overhanging shed, and behind this, senseless, suffocated, helplessly bound, two other forms. Thrusting the sacks aside, the troopers seized and dragged forth their hapless fellow-creatures. Jarred by sudden pressure, a burning upright snapped. There was a crackling, crashing sound, and down came the rafters, sending another column of flame to light up the features of men rescued not an instant too soon from the death that awaited them.

"My God!" cried Sergeant Lee, "this is old Feeny,—and yet alive."

Together the two raised the senseless form, bore it out into the open space, laid it gently beside their first discovery, and ran back for the next, a big, heavy, bulky shape in loose and blood-stained garments. It took all their strength to lug it forth. Then the lieutenant bent by the side of the slowly recovering civilian.

"Are there any more we can reach?" he questioned eagerly, his heart beating madly.

"No,—too late!—others were inside when the roof fell in. More water,—more water!"

Sergeant Lee sprang to the *ollas*, gleaming there in the fire-light, and brought back a brimming dipper, holding it to the poor fellow's parched lips until he could drink no more, then slashing away the thongs with which he was bound.

"This is Greaser work," he cried. "How could they have left you alive? Where are Moreno's people? Who's done this, anyhow?"

"Pasqual Morales. Moreno was in it, too. 'Twas the paymaster they were laying for; but they've killed Ned Harvey and got his sisters,—old Harvey's children—from Tucson."

"What?" cried the officer, leaping to his feet. "Harvey's daughters here?—here? Man, are you mad?"

"It's God's truth! Oh, if I had a drop of the whiskey that's being burned in there! I'm nigh dead."

"Run to my saddle-bags, Lee; fetch that flask, quick; then call in the men and send one back to hurry up the rest. Where have they gone? What have they done with their captives?"

"God knows! I could hear them screaming and praying,— those poor girls! Mullan and the pay-clerk picked up Feeny after he was stunned and they rushed him back through here, where the paymaster had dragged himself, to where you found him. That—that's the paymaster you've got there. Then they tried to save a drunken soldier while all the gang seemed crowding after the safe and the girls, but they were shot down inside, and must have burned to death if they wasn't killed. Oh, God, what a night!" And weak, unstrung, unmanned, the poor fellow sobbed aloud.

At this instant there rode into the corral a couple of troopers.

"Lieutenant Drummond here?" cried one of them. "We've found a man out on the plain to the southeast, gagged and bound. Shall we fetch him in?"

"You go, Quinn, but get some one else to help you.

Patterson, your horse is fresh, gallop back on the trail. Tell Sergeant Meinecke to come ahead for all he's worth. Let the packs take care of themselves. Send Sergeant Lee in here to me again." Then with trembling hands the young officer turned his attention to his other patients. Severing the cords with his hunting-knife, he freed them from their bonds, then dashed water over their scorched and blackened faces, meantime keeping up a running fire of questions. Between his sobs, the young civilian told him that the outlaws had hitched in both teams and taken also the spare mules and the buck-board. They had lifted the Harvey girls into the Concord, the safe and Pasqual Morales into the paymaster's ambulance, while the wounded men and Moreno's people probably were put on the open wagon. Then they had all driven furiously away to the south, leaving only two or three men to complete the work at the ranch. Finding the paymaster and sergeant well-nigh dead, they had contented themselves with binding and leaving them to their fate, to be cremated when the roof of the shed came down. Then one of the gang whom he had once befriended in Tucson pleaded with his fellows to spare the life of the only one of the party left to tell the tale. Pasqual and the Mexicans were gone. Those who remained were Americans, judging by their speech, though two of them were still masked. "My name is Woods," said the poor fellow. "But that bandit had to beg hard. They were ready to murder anybody connected with the defence, for Ramon was killed and Pasqual shot through the leg. I did that, though they didn't know it. They bound and left me here, but made me swear I would tell Harvey and his friends when they got back that it was no use following; they had thirty armed men and three hours' start. They never thought of any one else getting here first. Oh, my God! who can break it to Mr. Harvey when he does come?"

And then Sergeant Lee came hurrying back, one or two men with him, and together they labored to restore to consciousness the paymaster, breathing feebly, and old Feeny, bleeding from a gash in the back of the skull and a bullet-hole through the body. For nearly quarter of an hour their efforts were vain. Meantime Drummond, well-nigh mad over the delay, was pacing about like a caged tiger. He set two of the men to work to hitch the bewildered little burros to the well-wheel and get up several huge bucketfuls of water against the coming of the troop. He ordered others to rub down his handsome sorrel, Chester, and the mounts of two of the advanced party. At last after what must have seemed an age, yet could not have been over thirty minutes from the time of their arrival, a soldier running in, said he could hear hoofs out on the plain, and at the same instant two men appeared lugging between them, bleeding and senseless, the ragged form of Edward Harvey.

Scratched, torn, covered with blood and bruises, and still unconscious though he was, Drummond knew him at a glance. They had met the previous year, and though only once it was enough. Men with young and lovely sisters are not soon forgotten. Kneeling by his side, the lieutenant sought anxiously for trace of blade or bullet. Rents there were many and many a bloody scratch and tear, but, to his infinite relief, no serious wound appeared. Still in deep swoon, his friend seemed to resist every effort for his restoration. The dash of water in his face was answered only by a faint shivering sigh. The thimbleful of whiskey forced between his lips only gurgled down his throat, and Drummond felt no responsive flutter of pulse. The shock to his system must indeed have been great, for Harvey lay like one in a trance. Drummond feared that he might never again open his eyes to light and home.

And then the weary troop came trotting into view, old Sergeant Meinecke in command. Halting and dismounting at his signal, the men stood silent and wondering at their horses' heads, while their leader went in to report to his commander. Drummond barely lifted his eyes from the pallid features before him.

"Unsaddle, sergeant; rub down; pick out the best and likeliest horses. I want twenty men to go on a chase with me. How soon can the packs get up?"

"They must be fully half an hour behind, sir."

"Sorry for that, sergeant. We've got to take at least four of them; load them up with barley, bacon, hardtack, ammunition. Kick off everything else. We'll feed and water here before starting, then we've got to ride like the devil. Send Trooper Bland here as soon as he has unsaddled. I want him to ride with me. He knows all the roads to the south."

Meinecke saluted in his methodical German fashion, turned away, and presently could be heard ordering "Unsaddle" and then shouting for Private Bland.

"Are there any of our men besides the farrier who have any knowledge of surgery?" asked the lieutenant of Sergeant Lee.

"They say Bland has, sir. I don't know any one else."

"Well, I've just sent for him. Mr. Harvey here doesn't seem to be wounded, yet it's impossible to bring him to. Give Woods a little more whiskey and see if you can get a word out of the major or Feeny."

But efforts with the half-suffocated men had no effect. The whiskey with Woods had better results. He presently ceased his shivering sobs and could answer more questions. Drummond begged for particulars of the capture, and these the man found it difficult to give. He was stationed at the back door, the corral side, he said, and hardly saw the final rush. But there was something so queer about it. There had been a few minutes' lull. Then Harvey and Feeny both began to talk excitedly and to call out that the "road agents" were running away, and then presently there came sound of galloping hoofs and cheering, and both the sergeant and Mr. Harvey had shouted that the troops were coming and rushed out to meet them,—"And the next thing I knew," said Woods, "was seeing Feeny flattened out on the ground and crawling on his hands and knees and the room filled with roughs, some Mexicans, some Yanks, and I slipped into the corral and saw one of them shoot Feeny as he was trying to crawl after me; and while they were swearing and searching for the safe and carrying it out, Mr. Dawes and Mullan managed, somehow, to help the paymaster out, and then went in after the other man." Then Woods could tell little more. One thing, he said, amazed and excited him so he couldn't believe his eyes, but he was almost ready to swear that the fellow Feeny ran to shake hands with was a soldier in uniform, and that he held Feeny's hand while another man came up behind and "mashed" him with the butt of his pistol, and that this fellow in soldier clothes was the man who afterwards shot Feeny as he was trying to crawl away.

Drummond looked around at the man incredulous,—almost derisive. The story was improbable, too much so to deserve even faint attention. Just then Meinecke came back and, precise as ever, stood attention and saluted.

"Herr Lieutenant, Private Bland is not with my party at all, sir."

"Did you leave him back with the packs?"

"No, sir; the men say he wasn't with us all night. He rode ahead with the lieutenant until we came to Corporal

Donovan's body."

"He's not been with me since," exclaimed the lieutenant. "Sergeant Lee, ask if any of the men have seen him."

Lee was gone but a moment, then came back with grave face and troubled eyes, bringing with him a young trooper who was serving his first enlistment.

"Private Goss, here, has a queer story to tell, sir."

"What do you know? What have you seen?" asked Drummond.

"Why, sir, right after Sergeant Lee caught sight of the fire and sung out that it was Moreno's I was back about a couple of rods looking for my canteen. I was that startled when they found Corporal Donovan dead that I dropped it, and all of a sudden somebody comes out past me leading his horse, and I asked him what he had lost, and he said his pipe, and passed me by, and I thought nothing more about it,—only no sooner did he get out into the dark where I couldn't see him than I heard all of a sudden a horse start at full gallop right over in this direction, and now I think of it it must have been Bland, for it was him that passed me, sir,—sneaking out like."

Drummond sprang to his feet.

"What say you to this, sergeant? Do you believe,—do you think it possible that Bland has deserted and joined these outlaws?"

"I don't know what to think, sir, but I haven't forgotten what Feeny said of him."

"What was that?"

"That he had too smooth a tongue to have led a rough and honest life; that if he was a Texan as he claimed, Texas people had learned to talk a different lingo since he was stationed among them with the old Second Cavalry before the war, and that he wished he'd been there at Lowell when the adjutant accepted those letters from former officers of the regiment as genuine. Bland would never show them to Feeny. Said he had sent 'em all to his home in Texas. That was what made bad blood between them."

"By heaven! and now to think that one of our troop—'C' troop—should have been engaged in this outrage! But we'll get them, men," said Drummond, straightening up to his full height and raising his gauntleted hand in air. "They can't go fast or far with those wagons such a night as this. They'll strike the foot-hills before they've gone ten miles, then they'll have to go slow. We'll catch them before the sun is up, and, by the God of heaven, if Bland is with them, I'll string him to the highest tree we can find."

"There's more than him that'll be strung up," growled a grizzled old trooper in an undertone. "The gang that murdered Pat Donovan will find scant mercy in this crowd."

"Ay, ay," said another, "and there's more than Pat Donovan to be scored off. Look yonder." For at the instant one of the packers came leading into the corral a resisting mule, at sight of whose burden many of the horses started in fear. It was the lifeless body of Donovan's companion, the soldier who had escaped the assassin's bullet when "Patsy" fell only to be overtaken and cut down half-way to Moreno's.

"It's the bloodiest night I've known even in Arizona," said Lee to his young leader. "The paymaster and Mr. Harvey about as good as dead, old Feeny dying, most like, the clerk and Mullan and some other trooper of the escort burned to ashes in that hell-hole there, and Donovan and this last one—some of our fellows think is Flynn, from 'F' troop—shot to death. It's worse than Apache, lieutenant, and there'll be no use trying to restrain our fellows when we catch the blackguards."

Quarter of an hour later, leaving half a dozen soldiers under an experienced sergeant to guard the packs, the wounded, and the non-combatants at the smouldering ruins of the ranch, with barely a score of seasoned troopers at his back, Lieutenant Jim Drummond rode resolutely out towards the southern desert, towards the distant line of jagged mountains that spanned the far horizon. The false and fatal blaze at the Picacho had utterly disappeared, and all was darkness at the west. The red glow of the smouldering embers behind was no longer sufficient to light their path. Straight away southward led the wheel-tracks, first separate and distinct, but soon blending, as though one wagon had fallen behind and followed the trail of the bolder leader in the first. Straight away after them went the ruck of hoof-tracks, telling plainly that for a time at least the gang had massed and was prepared to guard its plunder. Stop to divide it was evident they dared not, for they had not with them the implements to break into the safe, and all their searching and threatening had failed to extract from the apparently dying paymaster any clue as to what he had done with the key. Stick together, therefore, they undoubtedly would, reasoned the lieutenant, and all their effort would be to reach some secure haunt in the Sierras, and there send back their demand for ransom. Twenty-five thousand dollars in cash and George Harvey's precious daughters! It was indeed a rich haul,—one that in all the dread history of the Morales gang had never been equalled. Even had they failed to secure the safe the richer booty was theirs in having seized the girls. But few people in Arizona—as Arizona then was constituted—would make great effort to overhaul a gang of robbers whose only victim was Uncle Sam and "his liveried hirelings." Nobody in Sonora would fail to regard them with envious eyes; but in the deed of rapine that made them the captors and possessors of those defenceless sisters each man had put a price upon his head, a halter round his neck, for "Gringo" and "Greaser," American and Mexican alike, would spring to arms to rescue and avenge.

As the rearmost of the little party of pursuers disappeared in the darkness and the wearied pack-mules went jogging sullenly after, urged on by the goad of their half-Mexican driver, the sergeant left in charge of the detachment at the corral looked at his watch and noted that it was just half-past two o'clock. The dawn would be creeping on at four.

Wearied as were his men he did not permit them all to rest. The condition of his wounded and the instructions left him by Lieutenant Drummond made it necessary that they should have constant attention. It was sore trouble for him to look at the old paymaster, whose life seemed ebbing away, lying there so pallid and moaning at times so pitifully, but Feeny lay torpid, breathing, yet seeming to suffer not at all. Both were in desperate need of surgical attendance, but where could surgeon be found? The nearest was at Stoneman, the little cantonment across the Christobal, thirty miles to the east; and though a gallant fellow had volunteered to make the ride alone through the Apache-infested pass and carry the despatch that Drummond had hurriedly pencilled, there was no possibility of doctors reaching them before the coming night, and the thought of all they might have to suffer through the fierce white heat of the intervening day was one that gave the sergeant deep concern. Then, too, who could say whether the solitary trooper would succeed in running the gauntlet and making his way through? He was a resolute old frontiersman, skilled in Indian warfare, and well aware that his best chance was in the dark, but speed as he might the broad light of day would be on him long before he could get half-way through the range. The stage from the west would probably come along about sunset, but nothing could be hoped for sooner. No troops were nearer than the Colorado in that direction except the little signal-post at the Picacho. Corporal Fox and two men had been sent thither to inquire what the signal meant, and it would soon be time for them to come riding in with their report. How he wished Wing were here! Wing knew something about everything. He was an expert veterinarian, something of a doctor, knew more of mineralogy than all the officers put together, and could speak Spanish better than any man in the regiment. When it became necessary to have a signal-station at the peak and it was found that no one knew anything about the business, Wing got one of the old red manuals, studied the system, and inside of a week was signalling with the expert sent down from San Francisco.

The interior of the ranch was still a smouldering furnace as four o'clock drew nigh. Woods, weak and exhausted, had fallen into an uneasy sleep. The trooper detailed to watch over old Plummer and Feeny and bathe their faces with cool water was nodding over his charge. Here and there under the shed on the north side which the flames had not reached the men were dozing, or in low, awe-stricken tones, talking of the tragic events of the night. Near the east gate, reverently and decently covered with the only shroud to be had, the newest of the saddle-blankets, lay the stiffening remains of poor Donovan and his comrade. Lurking about the westward end of the enclosure, their beady eyes every now and then glittering in the fire-light, the Mexicans, men and boy, were smoking their everlasting *papellitos*, apparently indifferent to the fate that had deprived them of home and occupation. One of the troopers had burrowed a hole in the sand, started a little cook fire, and was boiling some coffee in a tin quart mug. Overhead and far down to the horizon, on every side the stars shone and sparkled through the vaporless skies. Eastward towards the Christobal they were just beginning to pale when a faint voice was heard pleading for water. Sergeant Butler sprang from his seat and hastened to where he had left Mr. Harvey but a few minutes before, still in deep and obstinate swoon.

"Water is it, sir? Here you are! I'm glad to see you picking up a little. Mr. Drummond left this for you, too, sir. He said you would maybe need it." And the sergeant raised the dizzy head and held a little flask to Harvey's lips.

"Where is he?" at last the sufferer was able to gasp.

"Overhauling the outlaws, hand over fist, by this time, sir. He has twenty good men at his back, and we'll have the ladies safe to-night,—see if we don't."

"Oh, God!" groaned the stricken brother, burying his face in his arms as the recollection of the fearful events of the night came crowding upon him. For a moment he seemed to quiver and tremble in every limb, then with sudden effort raised his head and turned again, the blood trickling anew from a gash in his face as he did so.

"Give me more of that," he moaned, stretching forth a trembling hand. "More water, too. Lend me a horse and your carbine. I must go! I *must* go!" But there his strength failed him, and grasping wildly at empty air, poor Harvey fell heavily back before the sergeant could interpose an arm to save.

"Don't think of it, sir; you're far too weak, and you're not needed. Never fear, the lieutenant and 'C' troop will do all that men can do. They'll bring the ladies safely back as soon as they've hung what's left of that murdering gang.—Hello!

Charles King

That you, Fox?" he shouted, springing up as two or three horsemen came spurring in.

"It's I,—Wing," was the answer in ringing tones. "Fox is coming slower. Quick now. Is it so that that gang has run off the young ladies?"

"It's God's truth. Here's Mr. Ned Harvey himself."

In an instant Wing was kneeling by the side of the prostrate man.

"Merciful heaven, my friend, but they've used you fearfully! They only bound and held me till Jackson got back from Ceralvo's a couple of hours ago. Are you shot,—injured?"

"No, no," groaned Harvey. "But I am broken, utterly broken, and my sisters are in the hands of those hounds."

"Never worry about that, man. I know young Drummond well. There isn't a braver, better officer in the old regiment if he is but a boy. He'll never drop that trail till he overtakes them, and by the time he needs us, old Pike here and I will be at his side. Thank the Lord, those louts were frightened off and never took our horses. They're fresh as daisies both of 'em. Cheer up, Mr. Harvey. If hard riding and hard fighting will do it, we'll have your sisters here to nurse you before another night.—Come, Pike," he cried, as he vaulted into saddle. "Now for the liveliest gallop of your lazy, good-for-nothing life. Come on!"

VII

A new May morning was breaking, its faint rosy light warming the crests of the Santa Maria, when Lieutenant Drummond signalled "halt" to his little band, the first halt since leaving Moreno's at half-past two. Down in a rocky canon a number of hoof-prints on the trail diverged to the left and followed an abrupt descent, while the wagons had kept to the right, and by a winding and more gradual road seemed to have sought a crossing farther to the west. It was easy to divine that, with such elements in the gang, there had been no long separation between the horsemen and the treasure they were guarding, and, eager as he was to overtake the renegades, Drummond promptly decided to follow the hoof-tracks, rightly conjecturing, too, that they would bring him to water in the rocky tanks below. Dismounting and leading his big sorrel, he sprang lightly from ledge to ledge down what seemed a mere goat-trail, each man in succession dismounting at the same point, and, with more or less elasticity, coming on in the footsteps of his leader. The faint wan light of early dawn was rendering neighboring objects visible on the sandy plain behind them, but had not yet penetrated into the depths of the gorge. Lying far to the west of the Tucson road, this was a section of the country unknown to any of the troop, and with every prospect of a broiling ride across the desert ahead so soon as the sun was up, no chance for watering their horses could be thrown away. Just as he

Charles King

expected, Drummond found the descent becoming more gradual, and in a moment or two the bottom of the dark rift was found, and presently, keeping keen lookout for the reflection of the stars still lingering overhead, the leading men were rewarded, and halted at the edge of a shining pool of clear, though not very cool, water, and the horses thrust their hot muzzles deep into the wave. Here, shaded by the broad-brimmed hats of white felt, such as the Arizona trooper of the old days generally affected, a match or two was struck and the neighborhood searched for "sign." The rocks around the tank were dry, the little drifts of sand blown down from the overhanging height were smooth. Whatsoever splashing had been done by the horses of the outlaws there had been abundant time for it to evaporate, therefore the command could not thus far have gained very rapidly on the pursued. But Drummond felt no discouragement. Up to this point the way had been smooth and sufficiently hard to make wheeling an easy matter. The wagons had been lugged along at brisk trot, the attending cavaliers riding at lively lope. Now, however, there would be no likelihood of their making such time. The ambulance could only go at slow walk the rest of the way, and the guards must remain alongside to protect the stolen funds, not so much from envious outsiders as from one another. Pasqual Morales showed his accustomed shrewdness when he forbade that any one should try to burst into the safe and extract the money, for well he knew that if divided among the men there would be no longer a loadstone to hold them together, to call for their fiercest fighting powers if assailed. The instant the money was scattered the gang would follow suit, and he be left to meet the cavalry single-handed.

The horses of the little detachment were not long in slaking their thirst. The noiseless signal to mount was given, and, following in the lead of their young lieutenant, the troopers rode silently down the winding cañon, Drummond and

Sergeant Lee bending low over their chargers' necks to see that they did not miss the hoof-prints. Little by little the light of dawn began to penetrate the dark depths in which they were scouting, and trailing became an easier matter. Presently the sergeant pointed to the face of the opposite slope, now visible from base to summit where an abrupt bend threw it against the eastern light.

"Yonder's where the ambulance came down, sir."

"I see, and we can't be far from where it crossed. Trot ahead and take a look. Let Patterson go with you. If you find a chance for short-cuts, signal."

Another half-hour passed away and still the trail led along this strange, rock-ribbed groove in the desert, the dry bed of some long-lost stream. When first met it seemed to be cutting directly across their line of march, now it had turned southward, and, for several miles ahead, south or west of south was its general course. The light was now broad and clear, though the sun had not yet peeped across the mountain range to their left. The pace was rapid, Drummond frequently urging his men to the trot or canter. Out to the front four or five hundred yards, often lost to view in the windings of the way, Sergeant Lee with a single trooper rode in the advance, but not once had he signalled a discovery worth recording. Both wagon and hoof-tracks here pursued a common road. It was evident that some horsemen had found it necessary to ride alongside. It was evident, too, that the outlaws were travelling at full speed, as though anxious to reach some familiar lair before turning to face their expected pursuers. Every one in the gang, from Pasqual down to their humblest packer, well knew that it could not be long before cavalry in strong force would come trotting in chase. The squadron at Stoneman would surely be on the march by the coming sunset. As for "C" troop, they had little to fear.

Pasqual laughed with savage glee as he thought how he had lured them in scattered detachments far up to the Gila or over to the Christobal. No need to fear the coming of the late escort of the paymaster. By this time those not dead, drugged, or drunk were worn out with fatigue. Over the body of his bandit brother, the swarthy Ramon, he had fiercely rejoiced that seven to one he had avenged his death, and Pasqual counted on the fingers of his brown and bloody hand the number of the victims of the night. Donovan and his fellow-trooper killed on the open plain. The paymaster and his clerk, Mullan and the other soldier, dead in their tracks and burned to ashes by this time, and, best of all, "that pig of a sergeant," as Moreno called him, that hound and murderer, Feeny,—he who had slain Ramon,—bound, gagged, and left to miserable death by torture. Indeed, as he was jolted along in the ambulance, groaning and cursing by turns, Pasqual wondered why he had not insisted that Harvey, too, should be given the *coup de grace* before their start. It was an unpardonable omission. Never mind! There in the brand-new Concord that came clattering along there was booty that outrivalled all. There was wealth far exceeding the stacks of treasury notes,—old Harvey's daughters,—old Harvey's daughters. It was with mad, feverish joy that when at last the sun came pouring in a flood of light over the desert of the Cababi he listened to the report of a trusted subordinate.

"I could see every mile of the road with my glasses, *capitan*, from the cliff top yonder—every mile from Moreno's to where we struck the canon. There isn't a sign of dust,—there isn't a sign of pursuing party."

"*Bueno!* Then we rest when we reach the cave. This is even better than I hoped."

But there were two elements in the problem Capitan Pasqual had failed to consider,—Lieutenant Drummond's scout in the

Christobal, Cochises's band of Chiricahuas in the Santa Maria. Who could have foreseen that the little troop, finishing its duties at the northern end of the range and about turning south to re-scout the Santa Maria, had ridden out upon the plain, summoned by the beacon at Picacho Pass, and less than two hours after their hurried start from the burning ruins at Moreno's were speeding on their trail? The best field-glasses ever stolen from the paternal government could not reveal to the fleeing outlaw that, only two or three miles back in the dim recesses of the crooked gorge, the blue-coats were following in hot pursuit. Who could have dreamed that a band of Apaches, cut off from their native wilds by detachments from Bowie, Lowell, and Crittenden, and forced to make a wide *detour* to the southwest, had sought refuge in the very gorge of the Cababi whither Pasqual with all speed was urging his men?

"We rest when we reach the cave."

Ah, even the torment of his wound could not have wrung from the robber chief this longed-for order had he dreamed what was coming at his back.

"How are the girls getting on?" he asked of his hot and wearied aide. "Are they tranquil now?"

"They have to be," was the grim reply. "The little one dare not open her eyes, and Sanchez has his knife at the elder's throat."

And the sunrise had brought with it new inspiration,—new purpose to those who came trotting to the rescue. Just as the cliffs on the western side were tipped and fringed with rose and gold, Sergeant Lee, riding rapidly far ahead from point to point, always carefully peering around each bend before signalling "come on," was seen suddenly to halt and throw himself from his horse. The next instant he stood erect, waving some white object high in air. Spurring forward, Drummond joined him.

"A lady's handkerchief, lieutenant," he quietly said. "They seem to have halted here a moment: you can tell by the hoof-prints. One of their number rode over towards that high point yonder and rejoined them here. I don't believe they are more than half an hour ahead."

Drummond reverently took the dainty kerchief, hurriedly searched for an initial or a name, and found the letters "R. H." in monogram in one corner.

"Push on, then, Lee! Here, one more of you,—you, Bennet, join the sergeant. Look alive now, but do not let yourselves be seen from the front."

Then as they hastened away he stowed the filmy trifle in the pocket of his blouse, and, drawing his Colt from the holster, closely inspected its loaded chambers. Only a boy, barely twenty-three, yet rich in soldierly experience already was Drummond. He had entered the Point when just seventeen. His father's death, occurring immediately before the memorable summer of their first class camp, had thrown him perforce into the society of the so-called bachelor club, and he was graduated in the June of the following year with a heart as whole as his physique was fine. But there were some cares to cloud his young life in the army,—a sister whose needs were many and whose means were few. He found that rigid economy and self-denial were to be his portion from the start, and was not sorry that his assignment took him to the far-away land of Arizona, where, as his new captain wrote him, "you can live like a prince on bacon and *frijoles*, dress like a cow-boy on next to nothing or like an Apache *in* next to nothing, spend all your days and none of your money in mountain scouting, and come out of it all in two or three years rich in health and strength and experience and infinitely better off financially than you could ever have been anywhere else. Leave whiskey and poker alone and you're all right."

He *had* left whiskey and poker alone, severely alone. He had sought every opportunity for field service; had shown indomitable push, pluck, and skill in pursuit of Apaches and cool courage in action. He had been able to send even more than was needed, or that he had hoped, to his sister's guardian, and was proud and happy in the consciousness of a duty well done. There were no young girls in the scattered garrisons of those days, no feminine attractions to unsettle his peace of mind. The few women who accompanied their lords to such exile as Arizona were discreet matrons, to whom he was courtesy itself on the few occasions when they met, but only once had he been brought under the influence of girlish eyes or of girlish society, and that was on the memorable trip to San Francisco during the previous year when he had had the great good fortune to be summoned as a witness before a general court-martial convened at the Presidio. He had been presented to the Harvey sisters by the captain of the "Newbern" and would fain have shown them some attention, but there had been much rough weather in the Gulf which kept the girls below, and not until after passing Cape San Lucas and they were steaming up the sunny Pacific did he see either of them again. Then one glorious day the trolling-lines were out astern, the elders were amidship playing "horse billiards," and "Tuck," the genial purser, was devoting himself to Paquita, when Drummond heard a scream of excitement and delight, and saw the younger sister bracing her tiny, slender feet and hanging on to a line with all her strength. In an instant he was at her side, and together, hand over hand, they finally succeeded in pulling aboard a beautiful dolphin, and landed him, leaping, flapping, splashing madly about, in the midst of the merry party on the deck. It was the first time Ruth had seen the gorgeous hues of this celebrated fish, and her excitement and pleasure over being heralded as its captor were most natural. From that time on she had pinned her girlish faith to the coat-sleeve of the tall, reserved young cavalryman. To him she was a child, even younger by a year than the little sister he had left, and of whom he soon began to tell her. To her he was a young knight-errant, the hero of a budding maiden's shyest, sweetest, fondest fancy, and ere long the idol of the dreams and thoughts she dared not whisper even to herself. Paquita, with the wisdom of elder sisterhood, more than half believed she read the younger's heart, but wisely held her peace. No wonder the little maid had so suddenly been silenced by the announcement at the pass that that very night she might again see the soldier boy to whom, in the absence of all others, her heart had been so constant. No wonder the ride forward to Moreno's was one of thrilling excitement and shy delight and anticipation; no wonder her reason, her very life, seemed wrecked in the tragic fate that there befell them.

And now as he rode swiftly in pursuit Drummond was thinking over the incidents of that delightful voyage, and marvelling at the strange fate that had brought the Harvey girls again into his life and under circumstances so thrilling. Never for an instant would he doubt that before the sun could reach meridian he should overtake and rescue them from the hands of their cowardly captors. Never would he entertain the thought of sustained defence on part of the outlaw band. Full of high contempt for such cattle, he argued that no sooner were they assured that the cavalry were close at their heels than most of their number would scatter for their lives, leaving Pasqual to his fate, and probably abandoning the wagons and their precious contents on the road. A sudden dash, a surprise, would insure success. The only fear he had was that in the excitement of attack some harm might befall those precious lives. To avert this he gave orders to be passed back along the column to fire no shot until they had closed with the band, and then to be most careful to aim wide of the wagons. Every man in the little troop well knew how much was at stake, and men, all mercy to their beasts at other times, were now plying the cruel spur.

Five, six o'clock had come and gone. The chase was still out of sight ahead, yet every moment seemed to bring them closer upon their heels. At every bend of the tortuous trail the leader's eye was strained to see the dust-cloud rising ahead. But jutting point and rolling shoulder of bluff or hill-side ever interposed. Drummond had just glanced at his watch for perhaps the twentieth time since daybreak and was replacing it in his pocket when an exclamation from Sergeant Meinecke startled him.

"Look at Lee!"

The head of column, moving at the moment at a walk to rest the panting horses, had just turned a rocky knoll and was following the trail into a broader reach of the canon, which now seemed opening out to the west. Instead of keeping in the bottom as heretofore, the wagon-track now followed a gentle ascent and disappeared over a spur four hundred yards ahead. Here Lee had suddenly flung himself from his horse, thrown the reins to Patterson, and, crouching behind a bowlder, was gazing eagerly to the front, while with hat in hand he was signalling "Slow; keep down." Up went Drummond's gauntlet in the well-known cavalry signal "Halt." Then, bidding Meinecke dismount the men and reset blankets and saddles, the young officer gave "Chester" rein and was soon kneeling by the side of his trusty subordinate.

Lee said no word at all, simply pointed ahead.

And here was a sight to make a soldier's pulses bound. Not a quarter-mile away the rocky, desolate gorge which they had been following since dawn opened out into a wide valley, bounded at the west by a range of rugged heights whose sides were bearded with a dark growth of stunted pine or cedar. On each side of their path a tall, precipitous rock stood sentry over the entrance and framed the view of the valley beyond. For full a mile ahead the trail swept straight away, descending gently to the valley level, and there, just pushing forth upon the wide expanse, with dots of horsemen on flank and front and rear, dimly seen through the hot dust-cloud rising in their wake, were the three wagons: the foremost, with its white canvas top, was undoubtedly the new Concord; the second, a dingy mustard-yellow, the battered old ambulance of the paymaster; the third and last, with no cover at all, Moreno's buck-board. It was what was left of the notorious Morales gang, speeding with its plunder to some refuge in the rocky range across the farther valley.

Somewhere in the few evenings Drummond had spent in the garrisons of Lowell, Bowie, or Stoneman, he had heard mention of a mysterious hiding-place in the Cababi Mountains whither, when pressed by sheriffs' posses, Pasqual Morales had been wont to flee with his chosen followers and there bid defiance to pursuit. And now the young soldier saw at a glance that the chase was heading along a fairly well defined track straight for a dark, frowning gorge in the mountains some three or four miles ahead of them. If allowed to gain that refuge it might be possible for Morales to successfully resist attack. With quick decision Drummond turned to the men still seated in saddle.

"Dismount where you are, you two. Reset all four saddles. We mount again here, sergeant, and we'll take the gallop as soon as the troop comes up."

"It's the only way, I believe, sir," answered Lee, his eyes kindling, his lips quivering with pent excitement. "Most of them will stampede, I reckon, if we strike them in the open. But once they get among the rocks, we'd have no chance at all."

Drummond merely nodded. Field-glasses in hand he was closely studying the receding party, moving now at leisurely gait as though assured of safety. His heart was beating hard, his blood was bounding in his veins. He had had some lively brushes with the Indian foe, but no such scrimmage as this promised to be. Never once had there been at stake anything to compare with what lay here before his eyes. Sometimes in boyish day-dreams he had pictured to himself adventures of this character,—the rescue of imperilled beauty from marauding foe; but never had he thought it possible that it would actually be his fortune to stand first in the field, riding to the rescue of the fair daughters of one of the oldest and most respected citizens of the Territory. In view of their peril the paymaster's stolen funds were not be considered. Jim Drummond hardly gave a single thought to the recapture of the safe. So far as he could judge the forces were about equally matched. Some saddle-horses led along after the wagons seemed to indicate that their usual riders were, perhaps, with others of the band, resting in the wagons themselves. Surprise now was out of the question. He would marshal his men behind the low ridge on which he lay, form line, then move forward at the lope. No matter how noiseless might be the advance, or how wearied or absorbed their quarry, some one in the outlaw gang would surely see them long before they could come within close range. Then he felt sure that a portion at least would stampede for the hills, and that he would not have to fight more than ten or a dozen. His plan was at all hazards to cut out, recapture, and hold Harvey's wagon. That, first of all; then, if possible, the others.

And now the time had come. In eager but suppressed excitement Meinecke and the men came trotting up the slope.

"Halt!" signalled Drummond; then "Forward into line," and presently the lieutenant stood looking into the sun-tanned faces of less than twenty veteran troopers, four sets of fours with two sergeants, dusty and devil-may-care, with horses jaded, yet sniffing mischief ahead and pricking up their ears in excitement. Drummond had been the troop leader in scout after scout and in several lively skirmishes during the year gone by. There was not one of his troopers whom he could not swear by, thought he, but then the recollection of Bland's treachery brought his teeth together with vengeful force. He found his voice a trifle tremulous as he spoke, but his words had the brave ring the men had learned to look for, and every one listened with bated breath.

"Our work's cut out for us here. Not more than a mile ahead now is just the worst band of scoundrels in all the West, and in their midst George Harvey's daughters. You all know him by reputation. They are in the white-topped wagon, and that is the one we must and shall have. Don't charge till I give the word. Don't waste a shot. Some of them will scatter. Let them go! What we want is their captives." With that he swung quickly into saddle.

"Ready now? No! don't draw pistol till you're close in on them, and no carbines at all this time. All right. Now— steady.—Keep your alignment. Take the pace from me. Forward!"

Up the gentle slope they rode, straining their eyes for the first sight of the hunted quarry, opening out instinctively from the centre so that each trooper might have fighting space. No squares of disciplined infantry, no opposing squadrons, no fire-flashing lines were to be met and overthrown by compact and instantaneous shock. It was to be a *melee*, as each trooper well knew, in which, though obedient to the general plan of their leader, the little detachment would be hurled forward at the signal "Charge," and then it would be practically a case of "every man for himself."

"I want you four fellows to stick close to me now," said Drummond, turning in saddle and indicating the desired set with a single gesture. "We move straight for the leading wagon. See that you don't fire into it or near it."

And these were the last instructions as they reached the ridge, and a hoarse murmur flew along the eager rank, a murmur that, but for Drummond's raised and restraining hand and Sergeant Lee's prompt "Steady there; silence!" might have burst into a cheer. And then the leader shook loose his rein, and just touching "Chester's" glossy, flank with the spur, bounded forward at the lope.

Out on the sandy barren, winding among the cactus plants, the weary mule-teams with drooping heads were tugging at the traces. Bearded men, some still with coal-blackened faces, rode drowsily alongside the creaking wagons. In one of these, the foremost, an arm in blue flannel suddenly thrust aside the hanging canvas curtain, and a dark, swarthy face, grooved from ear-tip to jaw with a jagged scar, appeared at the narrow opening.

"How much farther have we got to go, Domingo?"

"Only across this stretch, two—three miles, perhaps."

"Well, I want to know exactly. The sun is getting blazing hot and these girls can't hold out longer. Tell Pasqual I say there is more danger of his killing them with exhaustion than there is of their making way with themselves. Say the little one's about dead now. Here, take this canteen and get some fresher water out of the barrel under the wagon."

The fellow hailed as Domingo leaned to the right, took the canteen-strap, and then reined in his foaming broncho.

"Hold your team one minute, Jake," was the order to the driver, and, nothing loath, the mules stopped short in their tracks. Pasqual's ambulance was a few rods behind, and, to save time, Domingo dismounted and, placing the canteen under the spigot, drew it full of water, rewarded himself with a long pull, handed it up to the waiting hand above, and swung again in the saddle just as the second ambulance closing on the first came also to a willing halt, and the lead mules of the buck-board, whereon lay two wounded bandits, attended by Moreno's womenfolk, bumped their noses against the projecting boot.

"Some cool water, for God's sake!" gasped one of the prostrate men, and a comrade rode to the leading wagon to beg a little from Harvey's well-filled barrel. One or two men threw themselves from the saddle to the sands for brief rest. The dust-cloud slowly settled earthwards in their wake. Mules, horses, and men blinked sleepily, wearily. There hung in the heavy air a dull, low rumble as of thunder in the far-off mountains. There seemed a faint quiver and tremor of the soil. Was there distant earthquake?

Suddenly a wild yell, a scream from Moreno's buck-board, a half-stifled shriek from the white-covered wagon. The man in blue leaped forth and made a mad dash for the nearest riderless horse. Whips cracked and bit and stung. The maddened mules flew at their collars and tore away, the wagons bounding after them, and Pasqual Morales, thrusting forth his head to learn the cause of all the panic, grabbed the revolver at his belt with one fierce curse.

"Carajo!"

VIII

Whatever might have been his other moral attributes, Pasqual Morales had borne a name for desperate courage that seemed justified in this supreme moment of surprise and stampede. What he saw as he leaned out of the bounding vehicle was certainly enough to disgust a bandit and demoralize many a leader. Scattering like chaff before the gale his followers were scudding out across the desert, every man for himself, as though the very devil were in pursuit of each individual member of the gang. Eight or ten at least, spurring, lashing their horses to the top of their speed, were already far beyond reach of his voice. Close at hand, however, six or seven of the fellows, desperadoes of the first water, had unslung their Henry rifles and, blazing away for all they were worth, showed evidence of a determination to die game. Behind them, screaming at the tops of their shrill, strident voices, Senora Moreno and her daughter were clinging stoutly to the iron rail of their seats as the buckboard was whirled and dashed across the plain. Already both the wounded men had been flung helplessly out upon the sands, and, even as he looked, the off fore wheel struck a stout cactus stump; flew into fragments; the tire rolled off in one direction, and Moreno's luckless family shot, comet-like, into space and fetched up shrieking in the midst of a plentiful crop of thorns and spines. The husband and father, gazing upon the incident from over his shoulder and afar, blessed the saints for their beneficence in having landed his loved ones on soft soil instead of among the jagged rocks across the plain. But for himself the sooner he reached the rocks the better. A tall Gringo, who cast aside a dark-blue blouse as he rode, stooping low over his horse's neck, seemed bent on racing the late ranch-owner to the goal where both would be, and there was none to dispute with them the doubtful honor. Even those who had stampeded at the first yell of alarm were now reining back in broad, sweeping circle, unslinging the ready rifle and pouring in a long-range fire on the distant rank of cavalry, just bursting into the triumph of the charge. Here, there, and everywhere across the plain little puffs of blue-white smoke were shooting up, telling of the leaden missiles hurled at the charging line. But on like the wind came the troopers in blue, never pausing to fire a shot, their leader at racing speed.

Wounded though he was, Pasqual Morales was not the man to fail in the fight. Yelling orders and curses at his driver, he succeeded in getting him to control his frantic team just long enough to enable the outlaw captain to tumble out. Then away they dashed again, the stiffening body of Ramon and the weighty little safe being now sole occupants of the interior. In the mad excitement of the first rush two or three horses had broken loose, leaving their owners afoot, and believing that no quarter would be the rule, these abandoned roughs were fighting to the last, selling their lives, as they called it, as dearly as possible. From their rifles and from others the shots rained fast upon the troopers, but never seemed to check the charge. The rush was glorious. Drawing their revolvers now, for they carried no sabres, the soldiers fired as they rode down those would-be obstructers, and two poor wretches were flattened out upon the plain when the main body of the troop dashed by, making straight for the fleeing Concord with the white canvas top. Drummond had not fired at all. Every thought was concentrated on the occupants of the wagon. Every shot might be needed when he got to them. "Chester" was running grandly. The designated four who were to follow the lieutenant were already over a hundred yards behind when, from the trail of the ambulance, from a little patch of cactus, there came a flash and report, and the beautiful horse swerved, reeled, but pushed gamely on. Noting the spot, two of the following troopers emptied a cartridge into the clump, but left the lurking foe to be looked after later. They were too close to the Concord to think of anything else,—so close they could hear the cries and pleadings of a woman's voice, the terrified scream of another, and then, all on a sudden, "Chester" pitched heavily forward, and, even as the wagon came to a sudden stand, the gallant steed rolled over and over, his rider underneath him.

When Lieutenant Drummond regained his senses he found himself unable to believe them. Conscious at first only of being terribly bruised and shaken, he realized that he was being borne along in some wheeled vehicle, moving with slow and decorous pace over a soft yet unbeaten and irregular trail. Conscious of fierce white light and heat about him on every side, he was aware of a moist, cool, dark bandage over his eyes that prevented him from seeing. Striving to raise a hand to sweep the blinding cloth away, he met rebellion. A sudden spasm of pain that made him wince, the quick contraction of his features, the low moan of distress, were answered instantly by a most surprising wail in a sweet girlish voice.

"Oh, Fanny, see how he suffers! Can't something be done?"

And then—could he be mistaken?—soft, slender fingers were caressing the close-cropped hair about his temples. A glow of delight and rejoicing thrilled through his frame as he realized that the main object of the fierce and determined pursuit was accomplished, that the precious freight was rescued from the robber band, and that somehow—somehow he himself was now a prisoner.

Striving to move his head, he found it softly, warmly pillowed; but as he attempted to turn, it was held in place by two little hands, one on each side. Then as he found his voice and faintly protested that he was all right and wanted to look about him, another hand quickly removed the bandage, and Fanny Harvey's lovely face, pale and framed with much dishevelled hair, was bending anxiously over him; but a smile of hope, even of joy, was parting the soft lips as she saw the light of returning reason in his eyes. At this same instant, too, the hands that supported his face were suddenly drawn away, and his pillow became unstable. One quick glance told him the situation. The seats of the Concord had been lifted out, blankets had been spread within; he was lying at full length, his aching head supported in Ruth Harvey's lap. Fanny, her elder sister, was seated facing him, but at his side. No wonder Jim Drummond could not quite believe his senses.

It was Fanny who first recovered her self-poise. Throwing back the hanging curtain at the side, she called aloud,—

"Mr. Wing, come to us! He's conscious."

And the next instant the slow motion of the wagon ceased, the door was wrenched open, and there in the glowing sunshine stood the tall sergeant whom he last had seen when scouting through Picacho Pass.

"Bravo, lieutenant! You're all right, though you must be in some pain. Can you stand a little more? We're close to the caves now,—cool water and cool shade not five hundred yards ahead."

"How did you get here, sergeant?" Drummond weakly questioned. "Where are the others?"

"Followed on your trail, sir, Private Pike and I. Most of the men are gathering up prisoners and plunder. You've made the grandest haul in all the history of Arizona. I got up only just in time to see the charge, and Pike's now on his way back already with the good news. We are taking you and the ladies to the refuge in the rocks where Morales and all his people have hid so long. Old Moreno, with a lariat around his neck, is showing the way."

"Got him, did you? I'm glad of that. There was another,—a deserter from my troop; did you see anything of him?"

"I haven't heard yet, sir. One thing's certain, old Pasqual is with his hopeful brother in another if not a better world. 'Twas he that killed poor 'Chester,' the worst loss we've met. Not a man is hit, and by daybreak to-morrow Dr. Day from Stoneman will be here to straighten you out, and these young ladies' father here to thank you."

"Thank you, Mr. Drummond? Ah, how can he or I ever begin to thank you and your brave fellows half enough? I had lost all hope until that disguised bandit suddenly leaped from the wagon, and Ruth was swooning again, but she heard your voice before I did. 'Twas she who saw your charge." And Fanny Harvey's lips quivered as she spoke, and the voice that was so brave at the siege became weak and tremulous now.

Drummond closed his eyes a moment. It was all too sweet to be believed. His right hand, to be sure, refused to move, his left stole up and began groping back of his head.

"May I not thank my nurse?" he said. "The first thing I was

conscious of was her touch upon my forehead."

But the hands that were so eager, so active when their patient lay unconscious, seemed to shrink from the long, brown fingers searching blindly for them, and not one word had the maiden vouchsafed.

"I heard your voice a moment ago, Ruthie. Can't you speak to me now?" he asked, half chiding, half laughing. "Have you forgotten your friend Jim Drummond and the long, long talks we used to have on the 'Newbern'?"

Forgotten Jim Drummond and those long talks indeed! Forgotten her hero, her soldier! Hardly. Yet no word would she speak.

"The little lady seems all unstrung yet, lieutenant. Miss Fanny will have to talk for her, I fancy." And Wing's clear, handsome eyes were raised to Miss Harvey's face as he spoke in a look that seemed to tell how much he envied the soldier who was the object of such devoted attention. "Shall we move ahead? The others will join us later on."

But when a few minutes later strong arms lifted the tall lieutenant from the wagon and bore him to a blanket-covered shelter in a deep rocky recess where the sun's rays seemed rarely to penetrate, and a cup of clear, cool water was held to his lips, Drummond's one available hand was uplifted in hopes of capturing the ministering fingers. There was neither difficulty nor resistance. It was Sergeant Wing's gauntlet, and Wing's cordial voice again accosted him.

"Glad to see you so chipper, lieutenant. Now, I have some little knowledge of surgery. Your right arm is broken below the elbow, and you're badly shocked and bruised. I have no doubt the surgeon will be with us by this time to-morrow, but I can set that arm just as soon as I have looked the ground over and disposed of ourselves and our prisoners to the best advantage."

"How many prisoners have we?" asked Drummond.

"Well, as yet, only Moreno and his interesting family and two of their gang, who are very badly wounded. Some of the others were neither prompt nor explicit about surrendering, and the men seem to have been a trifle impatient in one or two cases. You should hear the old woman protesting to Miss Harvey her innocence and her husband's spotless character. You understand Spanish, do you not?"

"No, only the smattering we pick up at the Point and what 'broncho' Spanish I have added to it out here. Where did you learn it, sergeant? They tell me you speak it like a native."

Wing's sunburned face—a fine, clear-cut, and manly one it was—seemed to grow a shade or two redder.

"Oh, I have spoken it many years. My boyhood was spent on the Pacific slope. Pardon me, sir, I want to look more carefully after your injuries now."

"But the ladies, where are they?" asked Drummond, uneasily.

"Occupying the sanctum sanctorum, the innermost shrine among the rocks. This is a wonderful spot, sir. We might eventually have starved these people out if once they got here, but ten determined soldiers could hold it against ten hundred. I've as yet had only a glance, but the Morenos have been here before, it is most evident, for the senorita herself showed Miss Harvey into the cave reserved for the women. There they have cool water, cool and fresh air, and complete shelter."

And now, as with experienced hands the sergeant stripped off Drummond's hunting-shirt and carefully exposed the bruised and lacerated arm and shoulder, he plied his patient with questions as to whether he felt any internal pain or soreness. "How a man could be flattened out and rolled over by such a weight and not be mashed into a jelly is what I can't understand. You're about as elastic as ivory, lieutenant, and you have no spare flesh about you either. That and the good luck of the cavalryman saved you from worse fate. You've got a battered head, a broken arm, and had the breath knocked out of you, and that's about all. But we'll have you on your feet by the time the fellows come from Stoneman."

"But how about the young ladies?" again asked Drummond, wearily and anxiously, for his head was still heavy and painful and his anxiety great. He was weak, too, from the shock. "Won't they suffer meantime?"

"Well, they might,—at least Miss Ruth, the younger, might in the reaction after their fearful experience; but I'm something of a doctor, as I said, and I shall be able to prevent all that."

"How?"

"Well, by giving her something to do. Just as soon as they've had a chance to rest, both young ladies will be put on duty. Miss Ruth is to nurse you."

"Suppose she doesn't want to?"

"The case isn't supposable, lieutenant. She would have gone into hysterics this morning, I think, had she not been detailed, as a preventive, to hold your head. At all events, she quieted down the instant she was told by her sister to climb into the wagon again and sit still as a mouse and see that your face was kept cool and moist and shaded from the glare." And now Sergeant Wing's lips were twitching with merriment, and Drummond, hardly knowing how to account for his embarrassment, asked no more. His amateur surgeon, however, chatted blithely on.

"There's an abundant store of provisions here, dried meat, frijoles, chile, chocolate.—You shall have a cup in a moment.—There's ammunition in plenty. There's even a keg of mescal, which, saving your presence, sir, as I am temporary commander, shall be hidden before the men begin coming in with their prisoners. There's barley in abundance for horses and mules; water to drink and water to bathe in. We could hardly be better off anywhere."

Drummond looked curiously about him, so far as was possible without moving his pain-stricken head. He was lying in a deep recess in some dark and rocky canon whose sides were vertical walls. Tumbling down from the wooded heights above—rare sight in Arizona—a little brook of clear, sparkling water came brawling and plashing over its stony bed at his feet and went on down the gorge to its opening on the sandy plain. There, presumably, it burrowed into the bosom of the earth, for no vestige of running stream could the Cababi Valley show. The walls about him were in places grimy with the smoke of cook fires. Overhead, not fifty feet away, a gnarled and stunted little cedar jutted out from some crevice in the rocks and stood at the edge of the cliff. A soldier was clinging to it with one hand and pointing out towards the east with the other. Drummond recognized the voice as that of one of his own troop when the man called out,—

"Two of our fellers are coming with the old yellow ambulance, sergeant; but I can't see the others."

"All right, Patterson. Try to see where the rest have gone and what they're doing. I'll send the glass up to you presently. What I'm afraid of, lieutenant, is that in their rage over Donovan's death, and Mullan's, and all the devil's work done there at Moreno's, and your mishap, too, the men have become uncontrollable, and will never let up on the pursuit until they have killed the last one of that gang. These two who are coming in with the bodies of the Morales brothers probably have worn-out horses, or perhaps Lee ordered them to stay and guard the safe. The last I saw of any of the gang they were disappearing over the desert to the south, striking for Sonora Pass."

"I wonder they didn't all come in here," said Drummond.

"Well, hardly that, lieutenant. They knew they would be followed here, penned up, where their capture would only be a question of time. A hundred cavalrymen would be around them in a very few hours, and we could send to Lowell for those old mountain howitzers and just leisurely shell them out. Then, when they surrendered,—as they'd have to,—the civil authorities would immediately step in and claim jurisdiction, claim the prisoners, too. We'd simply have to turn them over to justice as a matter of course, and you know, and they know, that the only judge apt to sit on their case would be that of our eminent frontiersman and fellow-citizen,—Lynch. They are scattering like Apaches through the mountains and will reassemble and count noses later on. Thanks to you and 'C' troop, they have lost all they had gained and their leaders besides. No, sir, they won't stop this side of the Mexican line."

"There's one, Wing, I hope to heaven they'll never lose sight of till they run him down."

"Who's that, sir?"

"The fellow who was enlisted in 'C' troop last winter at Tucson and who deserted last night to join this gang. He drove for the stage company last year and was discharged. He gave his name as Bland."

"Bland! Henry Bland!" exclaimed Sergeant Wing, leaping to his feet in uncontrollable excitement. "Do you mean it, sir? Had he enlisted? Do you mean that he was the man Miss Harvey spoke of,—the disguised soldier she called him?"

And Drummond, amazed at Wing's emotion, gazed up to see the sergeant's features working almost convulsively, his face paling, his eyes full of intense anxiety.

"Why, I cannot doubt it, sergeant. He ran away from us on the discovery of Donovan's body and rode straight for Moreno's, beating us there probably by an hour or so, for no one happened to miss him."

Wing's hands were raised on high in a gesture almost tragic, then dropped helplessly by his side. With a stifled groan the tall soldier turned abruptly away and went striding towards the opening of the canon, leaving Drummond wondering and perplexed.

When, quarter of an hour later, the sergeant returned, bringing with him some improvised splints and bandages, and Drummond believed it his duty to make inquiry as to whether he knew Bland and what was the cause of his excitement, Wing turned his grave, troubled face and looked his young superior straight in the eye.

"Mr. Drummond, I have known that man for good and for ill many a long year. If our fellows have killed him, let his crimes die with him. If he is brought in alive,—brought to trial,—I may have to speak, but not now, sir. Bear with me, lieutenant,—not now."

Was Drummond dreaming? He could have declared that tears were starting in the sergeant's eyes as he turned hastily away, unable for the moment to continue the setting and bandaging of the broken arm.

"Take your own time, Wing," said the young officer, gently. "Speak or keep silent as you will. You have earned the right." And the sergeant mutely thanked him.

The primitive surgery of the frontier took little time, and, with his arm comfortably and closely slung, Drummond lay impatient for the coming of his men, impatient perhaps to hear a softer voice, to feel again the light touch of slender fingers, yet in his weakness and exhaustion dropping slowly off to sleep. All efforts to keep awake proved vain. His heavy eyelids closed, and presently he was in dreamland.

Meantime Sergeant Wing had busied himself in many a way. First he had gone to loosen old Moreno's bonds,—enough, at least, to relieve his pain yet hold him securely. The soldier sitting drowsily on the rock beside the prisoner gladly accepted permission to put aside his carbine and go to sleep.

"I'll watch him, Mat," said Wing. "You lie down there, Moreno, and see to it that you make no effort to slip a knot while I'm at work here. How far away is that ambulance now, Patterson?" he called to the man on lookout.

"Halted down at the edge of the plain, sergeant. That's where they struck water first, and I reckon they couldn't make up their minds to come farther. I can make out one or two of the fellows coming back far down the desert to the south. Horses played out probably."

"Anything to be seen across the valley along the trail we came?"

"Nothing, sir; not a puff of dust. But here's something I don't understand—off here in the range south of us—well up towards the top."

"What's that?" asked Wing, dropping the coil of lariat he held in his hand and looking quickly up.

"Well, it's more like signal-smoke than anything else. Just exactly such smoke as we have seen in the Chiricahua and Catarinas and—Well, just come up here with your field-glass, if you can, sergeant. I believe there's an answer to it way down to the southeast,—t'other side of the valley."

In an instant Wing turned. "Sorry for you, Senor Moreno," he grimly muttered. "But as only two men are with me and both are otherwise engaged, I'll have to secure you temporarily. It isn't pleasant, but it serves you right."

In vain the Mexican pleaded and protested. A rawhide *riata* was wound and looped about him in a few scientific turns and he was left reclining against the rock, conquered yet inwardly raging, while Wing stole in to Drummond's rude couch, slipped the field-glass from its case, then, with a longing look into the darker depths beyond, and a moment's hesitation, he stepped to the projecting rock that seemed to divide the cave into two apartments and called in lower tone, "Miss Harvey."

"Here, Mr. Wing. What is wanted?"

And at the instant, prompt, alert, even smiling, Fanny Harvey appeared before him. The pallor was gone. The dishevelled hair had been twisted into shape. Food, rest, relief from dread and misery, and that little appreciated beautifier, fresh water, had wrought their transformation here. Wing's handsome eyes glistened as he removed his hat.

"I have to go up to that point yonder a few minutes, leaving old Moreno alone, bound, to be sure, but his wife or daughter might slip out and release him. Will you have the goodness—to take this—and shoot him if they should make the attempt?" And he handed her his pistol.

"I'll see to it that no one interferes with him, Mr. Wing. What has happened? Are the others coming?" And she took the revolver, balancing it in her accustomed and practised hand. The admiration deepened in Wing's gaze.

"I see you handle a pistol as though you had used one. You're a true frontiersman's daughter. I'll have to be away for a few minutes. I'm going up to look from our rock above there. Some of our men, they say, are in sight slowly returning, and the paymaster's ambulance is only a mile away, probably waiting for the rest of the party. How is Miss Ruth?"

"Sleeping like a baby, bless her heart."

"Well, I have promised Mr. Drummond that she should be his nurse. I hope you will consent. He is sleeping, too. No fever yet, I am thankful to say."

"Ruth will be ready, and so will I, to help in any way we can. But when are you to have a rest, may I ask?"

"O-oh—by and by. Lee and the others must have theirs first. They have been in saddle much longer and farther than I. When is Miss Harvey to have *her* rest, may *I* ask?"

"We-l-l, I don't know. I'll say, 'perhaps by and by' too. Look! that man is calling you."

Whirling about, Wing saw his sentinel beckoning, and in a moment he went clambering up the rocky trail, active as a mountain Apache.

"What is it, Patterson?"

"It *is* signal-smoke, sir, across the valley. That ain't more than eight miles away, and down here in the range ain't more than six. What Indians could be out here, I would like to know? Do they grow everywhere in this infernal country?"

Wing took his glasses and long and earnestly studied the bluish-white clouds rising in puffs, faint and barely distinguishable in the opposite heights, then fixed his gaze upon the filmy column soaring up among the dark pines at the heart of the range to the southward. His face grew graver every minute.

"Stay here and watch," he said. "I must go and get those other men in with the ambulance. Of course if it is Apaches, they've sighted that party and the few men straggling back, and those signals mean, 'close on them.' I'll send the team right in and then ride and hurry the other fellows out."

The sun was retiring behind the Cababi Range as Wing went leaping down the trail.

"Sorry for you, Dick, old boy," he said to his horse, who was drowsing in the shade. "More work for us both now."

Never stopping to saddle, he leaped upon the bare, brown back and went clattering down the canon.

"Keep your eye on Moreno, there!" he shouted up to the lookout. "If he tries to slip away, shoot him."

Ten minutes' brisk gallop through the windings of the gorge brought him to the edge of the sandy plain. There, under a little clump of willows, was the ambulance, its mules unhitched and hoppled securely, nibbling placidly at such scant herbage as they could find. The horses of the two guards, unsaddled, were drooping in the shade, too tired to hunt for anything to eat.

"Saddle up, men. Hitch in and get that team to the head of the canon, lively now," was his brief order to the sleepy trooper who greeted him, carbine in hand.

"What's up, sergeant?" queried another, springing out from the willows. "Lee told us to wait here, or wherever we could find shade and water."

"Wait? How long and what for?"

"Blessed if I know how long. None of 'em ain't in sight from here coming back; but 'what for' is easy to answer. The paymaster's chest."

"The paymaster's chest?" cried Wing. "Why, isn't that here in the ambulance?"

"Not a hinge of it. Those Greasers swapped it onto an *apparejo* while we were all running for Harvey's daughters. The money's half-way to Sonora by this time."

IX

Peaceful as was his rest, Drummond slept only an hour or so. For months he had lived in the open air, "on the war-path" said his captain, a veteran who had won his spurs twice over in the war of the rebellion, and declared himself quite ready to take his ease now and let the youngsters see for themselves the hollowness of military glory. Weariness and physical exhaustion had lent their claims, and despite bruises and many a pang, despite the realization of the presence of the fair girls whom his dash and energy had rescued from robber hands, the young fellow had dozed away into dreamland. Why not? The object of his mission was accomplished. Fanny and Ruth Harvey were safe. All that was left for the party to do now was rest in quiet until another morn, then it would be quite possible to start on the return without waiting for the coming of their friends. Before sunset his men would be reassembled; they could have a long night's sleep, and with the rising of the morrow's sun, convoying their three wagons and their recaptured treasures, the little detachment would take the back track for the Tucson road, confident of meeting "old Harvey" and, probably, a doctor on the way. He himself, though most in need of surgical attention when they reached the caves, had such confidence in the skill of Sergeant Wing as to feel that his arm was set as perfectly as could be done by almost any other practitioner, and before dropping off to sleep had quite determined that he would make the morning march in saddle.

Still, he could not sleep for any great length of time. The instinct of vigilance and the sense of responsibility would not leave him. In his half-dreaming, half-waking state, he once thought he heard a light foot-fall, and presently as he dozed with eyelids shut there came a soft touch upon his temple. Lifting his hand he seized that of his visitor,—Fanny Harvey.

"Why are you not resting?" he asked, "and where is Ruth?"

"Ruth is sleeping, as we hoped you might be. 'Tired Nature's sweet restorer' is all you need, Mr. Drummond, yet you do not seem to have had more than a cat nap. Twice I have stolen in here to see you, and then, though I was fearful of waking you, you slept peacefully through it all."

"Well, I must have slept a couple of hours anyway, and I slept soundly until within the last few minutes. Have none of the men got back yet, Miss Harvey? Do you know what time it is? I suppose Wing is sleeping."

"Mr. Wing ought to be sleeping, but he isn't. The sentry— Patterson I think they call him—summoned him up to the lookout there in the rocks, oh, about an hour ago, and when the sergeant came back he mounted his horse and rode away down the canon. He said there was something requiring his attention. But you are to drink this chocolate and lie still."

Drummond slowly strove to rise. He was too anxious, too nervous, to remain where he was.

"And none of them have returned yet?" he asked. "I cannot understand that. No, please do not strive to detain me here. I'm perfectly able to be up and about, and if Wing is gone it's my business to look after things."

Over among the rocks across the narrow canon the first object to meet his gaze as he arose was Moreno, reclining there bound and helpless, while near at hand a soldier had thrown himself on his saddle blanket and was sound asleep. The plash of the waters in the brook, dancing and tumbling down the chasm, made sweet, drowsing music for his ears, a lulling, soothing sound that explained perhaps the deep slumber of his trooper friend.

"I heard Mr. Wing tell that man to lie down and sleep," said Miss Harvey, as the young officer's eyes seemed to darken with menace at the sight of a sentry sleeping on guard. "Moreno is securely tied, and both Patterson up there and I here are now his keepers. The senora and her daughter are in the other cave, forbidden to go near him."

Glancing up at the stunted cedar where Patterson stood faithful to his trust, Drummond saw that he was peering steadily southward through the black field-glasses.

"What do you see, Patterson?" he hailed. "Where is Wing? Any of the men coming back?"

"Wing has gone on down the valley, sir. Some of our fellows, two or three only, were coming back, but they didn't come fast enough to suit him. The ambulance will be here in a minute or two,—it's just below us down the canon now."

Indeed, almost at the moment the click of iron-shod hoofs was heard, and the dejected mule-team came into view around a jutting point, the dingy yellow ambulance jolting after them, one soldier in the driver's seat handling the reins, the other riding behind and leading his comrade's horse.

"Come up here to the mouth of the cave, Merrill," called the lieutenant. "You can unhitch and unharness just beyond; but

I want that safe unloaded and put in here."

"The safe's gone, sir."

"What?"

"The safe's gone, sir. We never got it. That's what took Sergeant Wing off down the valley, I reckon. I supposed you knew it, sir, and him, too, but he didn't. Those Morales fellows got away with it on burro-back while we were chasing the white wagon."

For a moment Drummond stood astounded.

"Man alive!" he at last exclaimed, "why was I not told of this? Get me a horse at once, Walsh," he ordered. "I'll take Patterson's. You two remain here and see that that old scoundrel don't get loose,—Moreno there,—and that no harm befall the ladies. I'll ride down after Wing."

"Oh, Mr. Drummond, you must not think of going," exclaimed Miss Harvey. "You're far too seriously hurt, far too weak, to attempt such a thing. Please lie down again. Surely Mr. Wing will do all that any man could do to recover the safe. All the others are in pursuit. They must have overtaken them by this time. Come; I am doctor now that he is away. Obey me and lie still."

Drummond's one available hand found itself clasped by warm, slender fingers. He would have drawn it away and striven to carry out his design, but a glance at his two troopers told him that they plainly and earnestly advocated Miss Harvey's view of the case. He was in no condition to make the attempt. And at the moment, too, even as he strove to release his hand, another voice was heard, almost imploring.

"Oh, don't let him go, Fan; don't let him try to ride!"

And turning suddenly at the sound, Mr. Drummond found Ruth Harvey standing close behind her sister, her eyes suffused, her cheeks blushing red. It was the first time he had seen her to speak to since they landed at the old wharf at San Francisco a year gone by, and for the moment he forgot the safe, the funds, the crippled arm, the bandaged head, and every other item that should have occupied his thoughts.

"Why, Ruthie, is this you? How you have grown!"

And then the imprisoned hand was released only to be transferred to the clasp and keeping of another. In her fear that her knight, her soldier, would leave them, and, wounded though he was, insist on attempting to follow his men in their pursuit, the shyness of maidenhood was forgotten. Ruth had seized and clasped the long, brown fingers, and Drummond forgot for the moment all thought of quitting her presence for the field.

And then having—as she supposed—won her point, and having caught the new light in his admiring eyes, it became necessary to struggle for the release of the hand she had so unhesitatingly used to detain him. This might have proved a difficult matter, judging from the expression in Drummond's face, but for a sudden hail from Patterson.

"Can the lieutenant come up here a moment? There's something going on down there I can't understand."

Old Moreno, whose bonds could not restrain his shifting, glittering eyes, glanced quickly upward. Then, as he caught a menacing look in the sunburned face of the Irish trooper Walsh, he became as suddenly oblivious to all earthly matters beyond the pale of his own physical woes. And now it was

Ruth's hand that would retain its clasp and Drummond's that was again struggling for release. In a moment the lieutenant stood under Patterson's perch.

"What did you see? What was it like? How far away?"

"Six or seven miles, sir. The valley is broad and open, and three of our fellows were riding slowly back on the west side, while Wing was galloping as though to meet them, and when they weren't more than a mile apart Wing's horse went down,—looks no bigger than a black speck,—and the other three sheered off away from the rocks on this side and seemed to be scattering apart."

The words were low spoken so as to reach only his ear. Now it was no easy scramble for a man in Drummond's condition to make, but it took him only a little time to clamber to Patterson's side.

"There's something back of all this, and you know it, Patterson. What Apache sign have you seen?"

"Smoke, sir, on both sides. But we agreed, the sergeant and I, that the young ladies mustn't be alarmed nor you aroused. Then he rode away to hurry in any of our fellows who were in sight and warn them to keep out from the rocks. What I'm afraid of is that they've been ambushed, or at least that the Indians have ambushed him. His horse is down, and those others you see are away out on the plain now. They're working around towards the horse as though he were lying behind it, and they appear to be firing mounted."

What was Drummond to do? To leave his charges here, unprotected, was out of the question. Fail to go, or send, to Wing's relief he could not. Decide he must and decide quickly.

"Patterson, that party of Apaches can't be over a dozen strong or they would have rushed out of their cover by this time, yet they are too strong and too securely posted to be driven by that little squad, especially if Wing is wounded. I can't shoot now, but I can ride and direct. Every man who can shoot may be needed here. You have four now and can stand off forty Apaches—Tonto or Chiricahua—in such a position as this, so I leave you in charge. You have everything to help you stand a siege. Now see to it that the ladies are kept well under cover, and I'll hurry back with Walsh and what men I can find."

Then down he scrambled, giving one look at Moreno and his sleeping guardian as he passed, then gave a low-toned order to Walsh.

"Saddle your horse again and ride just to the other side of that rock yonder and wait for me."

Well he understood that it would be impossible for him to ride away without Fanny Harvey's knowing that something of a serious nature was impending, and that he could not get away at all without their knowing it. What he desired was to conceal from them that there was any danger from Apaches.

Just as he expected, both girls were eagerly awaiting him at the entrance to the cave. His revolvers were in there beside the rude couch on which he had slept so peacefully.

"Now are you ready to return to hospital and proper subjection?" asked Miss Harvey, laughingly. "It is high time. What could have tempted you to climb to that high point?"

"Why, it's the first chance I've had of a look around," was the answer. "This is an awfully strong spot for a place of refuge. You are safe here, safer than anywhere between Yuma and

Tucson, now that the former possessors are scattered. But did you hear what took Wing off?"

"No, he didn't stop to explain matters. He simply dashed away without even a saddle. 'Something I must look after,' was all he vouchsafed to say."

"Well, the men just in tell me the paymaster's safe was spirited off. Confound that little green box of greenbacks! Some shrewd packer among Morales's people whisked it out of the wagon and onto a *burro*, and now we are all keen to get it back. Of course I can't sleep again until we know. Some of our people are coming slowly up the valley and Wing went on down to meet them."

But all the time he talked so airily with the elder sister, Ruth stood watching him with suspicious eyes.

"Mr. Drummond, please do not go," she broke forth. "You have no right to—now." And James, the dissembler, found himself trapped.

"Go I must, Ruthie," he said, with sudden change of manner. "I know you will not blame me or detain when I tell you, as I feel forced to tell you now, that Sergeant Wing is hurt. His horse has fallen with him far out on the desert. I'll be back and very soon."

Then with sudden impulsive movement he bent, kissed her forehead, and turned as suddenly away.

When the sisters looked into each other's eyes a moment later one face was blushing like the dawn, the other was pallid with a new and deep anxiety.

And now we, too, must follow Wing. He was a total stranger,

it is to be remembered, to the regiment when, after its years of battling in the Army of the Potomac, it was sent into exile on the far Pacific coast and speedily lost to sight in the deserts of Arizona. The type of non-commissioned officer most familiar to the rank and file as well as to their superiors was the old-fashioned "plains raised," "discipplin furst and rayson aftherwards" class of which Feeny was so prominent an exponent. Brave to rashness and faithful to the very death, they had reason to look for respect and appreciation. They were men whose only education was that picked up in the camps and campaigns of the famous old regiments to which, when mere recruits, they had been assigned. They were invaluable in the army, and would have been utterly misjudged and out of their element anywhere else. That "book learning" and soldiering could ever go hand in hand no man in the old dragoons would ever have believed for an instant. Such scholars as had drifted into the ranks were, as a rule, irreclaimable drunkards, lost to any chance of redemption at home, and only tolerated in the service in the rough old days because of their meek and uncomplaining performance of long hours of extra duty in the troop or regimental offices when, their whiskey and their money alike exhausted, they humbly went back to their desks, asking only to live in the hope of another drunk. Hundreds of the old dragoons could barely sign their names, many could only touch the pen when called upon to make "his (X) mark." "Another busted clerk" was the general expression when the young Californian came forward to enlist. Yet he was the picture of clear-eyed, athletic manhood, was accepted with much hesitancy by the officers and undoubted suspicion by the men, yet speedily proved a splendid horseman, scout, shot, and, as was the final admission, "all-round trooper," despite the fact that he was well educated and spoke Spanish like a native. Still, such was the prevailing faith, as it ever is among veteran soldiers, that the old style was the best, it was long before he won promotion. No one who has not known both can begin to imagine the difference between the army of a quarter-century ago and the army of to-day. Just as Feeny was a resolute specimen of the old, so was Wing a pioneer of his class in the new. At the moment when the latter struck spurs to the wearied flanks of poor Dick and called on him for one more effort, the stalwart and handsome sergeant sped away on the path of duty, confident of the fact that by this time every man in his own troop and every soldier who knew him at all would stake his last dollar on "Bob" Wing's tackling the problem before him as fearlessly and intelligently as any veteran in the regiment.

Having ordered the ambulance up the gorge, he himself spurred away to gather in all stragglers within reach, so as to reinforce the little garrison at the caves in the event of attack from the Apaches. To his practised eye no vestige of doubt remained as to the character and purpose of the signal-smokes. Not a moment was to be lost. Within that very hour, perhaps, unseen Indians would come skulking, spying, "snaking" upon their refuge, would be able, infallibly, to determine the number and character of its occupants, and, if their own force were considerable and that of the garrison weak, God alone could help those innocent women.

When last noted the westward signal was puffing slowly up into the cloudless sky from a point in the range perhaps six miles below Patterson's station in the rocks. The three wearied troopers dragging slowly back from the chase could be seen coming up the valley probably four miles away, some distance, therefore, ahead of the supposed position of the foe. Wing well knew with what goat-like agility the mountain Indians could speed along from rock to rock and still keep under cover, and every man who had served a month in Arizona could have predicted that if Indians in any force were within a day's march of those three stragglers ambush and death would be their fate, perhaps even when within view of their longed-for goal. That they had not seen the sign, that they were ignorant of the possible presence of Apaches in the range, was manifest simply because they rode close along under the foot-hills, often over the bowlder-strown outskirt of the *falda*, and, though still far from them, such was Wing's anxiety for their safety that he rode furiously along, signalling with his left hand as though to say "Keep out! Keep to your right! Don't go so close to the rocks!"

In this way, urging Dick to his speed and never thinking of his own safety, intent only on saving his comrades from possible death, believing, too, that no Apache could yet have worked his way so far up the range, Wing was riding, straight as the crow flies, from the little oasis at the mouth of the canon towards the ambling laggards to the south. His course led him along within a hundred yards of many a bowlder or "*suwarrow*," though his path itself was unobstructed. The sun had gone westering and he was in the shadow. Presently, however, as Dick panted painfully, heavily, up a very gentle slope and the sergeant came upon the low crest of a mound-like upheaval, he saw some four hundred yards ahead a broad bay of sunlight stretching in from the glaring sea to the east, and, glancing to his right, noted that there was a depression in the range,—something like a broad cleft in the mountains, possibly a pass through to the broader desert on the other side. He gave it little thought, however. There, only a mile or so away now, came his fellow-troopers, two in front, another lagging some distance behind, riding sleepily towards him and dangerously close to a number of sheltering rocks. Intent only on them and still wishing to attract their attention, he swung his broad-brimmed hat, waving it off to the left, but with no apparent result. Confound them! Were they sound asleep? Could they never be made to see? Poor Dick was able now only to strike a feeble canter, so utterly was he used up, and just when

Wing, looking only to the front, was thinking that he might as well discontinue the spur and let his poor horse rest, they labored forth from the sheltering shade full upon the tawny, sunlit sand. Then, while the sergeant's eyes were temporarily blinded by the glare, there came from the rocks to his right a sudden flash and report. He felt at the same instant a stinging pang in the leg. He had just time to grasp his own carbine and to attempt to swing off when the second shot echoed loudly from the rocks. He felt poor Dick start and swerve; he felt him going headlong, and the next thing he knew he was vainly striving to peer into the face of the evening sun from over the quivering body of his faithful friend, unable for the moment to see the faintest sign of an enemy, and then the blood came welling through the little hole in his worn cavalry trousers, midway between the hip-bone and the knee, and he knew he had received a serious, perhaps a desperate wound.

For the moment, therefore, he could do nothing more but look for succor. A glance down the desert told him his fellows were at last rudely awakened. True to the practice of the craft, the instant fire was opened from the rocks each man had put spurs to his horse and dashed away to a safer distance with such speed as was possible with their jaded mounts, each trooper warily scanning the dark line of the foot-hills in search of the foe and striving as he rode to unfasten the flap that held his carbine, in the fashion of the day, athwart the pommel of his saddle; and now, circling farther out upon the plain, in wide sweep, with carbines advanced, they were hastening to the succor of their comrade. Presently one of their number suddenly drew rein, halted his startled "broncho," aimed to the left of the horse's head and fired, then, cramming a cartridge into the chamber, came riding farther. The others, too, followed suit, shooting at some object apparently among the rocks in front of the sergeant's position. One of the men threw himself from his saddle, and kneeling on the sands drove two or three shots at long range. Eager to add his own fire to theirs, Wing pulled his hat-brim over his eyes, threw forward the barrel over the now stilled carcass of poor Dick, and peered eagerly up the ravine in search of some foe at whom to aim. Blindly he searched for dusky Apache skulking from rock to rock; there was no moving thing in sight. But what was this,—this object that suddenly shot out from behind a little ledge and, turning sharply to the left, went clattering into the depths of a dark and frowning gorge? Could he believe his eyes? Did the Chiricahuas, then, have horses and wear trooper hats? Bending low over his steed and spurring him to the uttermost exertion, a tall, even soldierly, form had darted one instant into view and then gone thundering out of sight. Up to this moment Wing never had lost full control of his faculties. Now his brain reeled. Before his eyes rose a dense cloud of mist rushing forth from the mountain-side. Bowlders, near at hand, took to waltzing solemnly with their neighbors, and when at last the foremost trooper flung himself from his horse and crept to the sergeant's side, while his comrades rode on, keeping vigilant watch against the appearance of other foe, Sergeant Wing was found lying beside his dead horse: he had swooned utterly away.

By and by, with anxious face and bandaged head and arm, Lieutenant Drummond came galloping down; Wing was then submitting to the rude bandaging of his leg and lying limp and weak, his head resting on Dick's stiffening shoulder. But Wing's eyes were covered by his gauntleted hand; he never looked up at his young commander, though he heard his anxious queries.

"Is he much hurt? Were there many of them?"

"Shot through the leg here, sir," answered the sturdy corporal, "and was in a dead faint when we got to him. I don't know how many there was of them, lieutenant; they skipped off the moment we opened fire."

"They couldn't have seen us coming, lieutenant," eagerly spoke a young recruit. "They must have thought the sergeant was alone, for when we charged they just lit out for all they were worth, didn't they, Mike?" he eagerly asked his comrade, an older trooper.

"Oh, shut up, Billy! There's nothing an Apache doesn't see, but we were too far off to tell how many there was. I only saw one as he lept away. Shure the sergeant was nearer,—he could have seen."

"Sergeant Wing, it is I, Lieutenant Drummond. Look up a moment if you can. You were close to them, how many did you see?"

"How many Indians, sir?" asked Wing, faintly.

"Yes, how many?"

A pause. Then at last,—

"I didn't see one, sir."

X

Another day had dawned and another patient was added to Miss Harvey's hospital list at the caves. The original plan of starting on the return soon after daybreak had now to be abandoned, as Drummond explained, because here was a man who could not stand the journey. Surely there would not be many hours before the relief party from Stoneman, following their trail, would come speeding to the rescue, bringing to the wounded the needed surgical skill and attention, bringing to the Harvey girls their devoted father. The only question in the young lieutenant's mind as the sun rose, a burning, dazzling disk over the distant mountains to the east, was, which will be first to reach us, friends or foes?

Wearied and shattered though he was and replete as the night had been with anxiety and vigil, Drummond climbed the goat-track that led to the sentry's perch feeling full of hope and pluck and fight. He and his men had divided the night into watches, one being awake and astir, not even permitting himself to sit a moment, while the others slept. The fact that he was able to send back to the caves, have an ambulance hitched in and driven down to where Wing lay wounded, and to bear him slowly, carefully, back to shelter, reaching the caves without further molestation before darkness set in, had served to convince the young commander that he could count on reasonable security for the night. Unless they know their prey to be puny and well-nigh defenceless, Apaches make no assault in the darkness, and so, with the coming of the dawn, he had about him fit for service a squad of seven troopers, most of them seasoned mountain fighters. His main anxiety now was for Wing, whose wound was severe, the bullet having gone clear through, just grazing the bone, and who, despite the fact that Fanny Harvey early in the night had every now and then crept noiselessly in to cool his fevered head, seemed strangely affected mentally, seemed unnaturally flighty and wandering, seemed oppressed or excited alternately in a way that baffled Drummond completely, for no explanation was plausible. Two or three times during the night he had been heard moaning, and yet the moment Drummond or, as once happened, Miss Harvey hastened to his side, he declared it was nothing. "I must have been dozing and imagined the pain was greater than it was." Awake and conscious, so stout a soldier as he would be the last to give way to childish exhibition of suffering, yet twice Drummond knew him to be awake despite his protestation of dozing, and he did not at all like it that Wing should bury his face in his arms, hiding it from all. What could have occurred to change this buoyant, joyous, high-spirited trooper all on a sudden into a sighing, moaning, womanish fellow? Surely not a wound of which, however painful, any soldier might be proud.

Somewhere along towards four o'clock, when it was again Patterson's watch and Drummond arose from his blanket after a refreshing sleep of nearly two hours and he and his faithful sentry were standing just outside the mouth of the cave, they distinctly heard the same moan of distress.

"Is there nothing we can do to ease the sergeant, sir?" whispered Patterson. "This makes the second time I have heard him groaning, and it's so unlike him."

"We have no opiates, and I doubt if he would use one if we had. He declares there is no intense pain."

"Well, first off, sir, I thought he was dreaming, but he was wide awake, and Miss Harvey came in only a moment after I got to him. Could those devils poison a bullet as they do their arrows, and could that make him go into fever so soon?"

"I hardly think so; but why did you say dreaming?"

"Because once it was 'mother' he called, and again—just now—I thought he said mother."

The lieutenant turned, looking straight at his soldierly subordinate.

"By Jove! Patterson, so did I."

There was a little stir across the canon. Moreno was edging about uneasily and beginning to mutter blasphemy at his bonds.

"That fellow begged very hard to be moved down into that wolf-hole of a place where the Mexican women are, lieutenant, with those two bunged-up bandits to take care of. Nice time we'd have, sir, if the three of them was able to move. The boys'd make short work of them now, the way they're feeling. I went in and took a look at those two fellows. One of 'em is a goner, sure, but they're dead game, both of 'em. Neither one has a word to say."

"No," answered Drummond, "they refused to give their names to me,—said it was no earthly consequence what name we put over their graves, the right set of fellows would be along after a while and do them all the honor they cared for. How were the Moreno women behaving?"

"The girl was asleep, I should judge, sir. The old hag was rocking to and fro, crooning to herself until one of the two—the live one, I should call him—hurled a curse at her in Spanish and told her to dry up or he'd kill her. All a bluff, for he can't move a peg."

"Watch them well, Patterson, all the same. Hush!"

Again from within the deep shelter of the rocky cave came the low moan of anguish,—

"Mother! mother! if you knew—"

"Here, Patterson, I can't stand this. I'm going in to him." And, picking up the dim lantern which he had taken from the Harvey wagon, Drummond stole in on tiptoe and knelt again beside his wounded comrade.

"Wing! sergeant! Look up, man. Speak to me. You must be in distress, mental or bodily. Do let me help you in some way."

For a moment no reply whatever. Wing's face was hidden. Then he looked gently upward.

"Lieutenant, I'm ashamed to be giving you so much trouble. Please go and lie down again, sir; you're worse hurt than I am,—only I suppose I get to dozing off and then turn on that side."

"No, it isn't that, sergeant. There's something wrong, and it has all come on you since yesterday morning. Where is your mother?"

Again Wing turned away, burying his face in his arms.

"Listen, sergeant; we hope to get you out of this by to-night. Dr. Gray ought surely to reach us by that time, and while we may have to keep up a field hospital here a day or two, my first duty will be to write and tell your mother how bravely you have served us, and she shall be told that you are wounded, but not in such a way as to alarm her."

Out came a restraining hand.

"Lieutenant, she must not know at all."

"Well, she can't, so far as I'm concerned, as I don't know her address. But think a moment; you know and I know—Hold on, wait!" And Drummond rose and tiptoed to a cleft in the rock through which shone a dim light; it was the entrance to the remote inner cave where the Harvey girls were sleeping. Assured that his words could reach there no listening ears, Drummond returned, kneeling again by the sergeant's side. "Just think, man; any moment after daybreak the Apaches may be upon us, and, who knows? it may be my last fight. Of course I believe that our fellows can stand them off until rescue comes, but a bullet may find me any moment, and then who is there to report your conduct and secure the recognition due you, or, if the doctor should be late in coming and fever set in and this wound prove too much for your strength, is there nothing that ought to be said to her for you?"

Again only painful silence. At last Wing spoke.

"I understand. I appreciate all you say. But I've got to think it over, lieutenant. Give me an hour or so. Don't ask me to tell you now."

"So be it, man. Now rest all you possibly can. It's almost day. The crags are beginning to light up back of us here already.

Yes, and the sentry's calling me now. I'll be back by and by. What is it, Patterson?" he whispered, going to the mouth of the cave.

"I've just come down from the tree up there, sir. You can see quite a ways down the range now, though the light is dim, and what I take to be a signal-fire leaped up not three miles below us, certainly this side of where Wing was shot."

"So soon? All right, then get back to the post just as quick as you can. I'll rouse the man who has slept longest. All must be astir in half an hour, but you keep watch there."

And half an hour later it is that, field-glass in hand, the young officer is there by Patterson's side, peering eastward almost into the eye of the sun, searching with anxiety inexpressible for any sign of dust-cloud rising along the trail on which they came, for the sight he has seen down the range, now brilliant in the morning light, has filled his heart with the first real dread it has yet known. In three places, not more than four or five miles apart, down along the sunlit side of this wild and picturesque mountain-chain, signal-smokes have been puffing straight up skyward, the nearest only a couple of miles from this lone picket post, but all on the same side of the valley.

Last evening the answer came from across the broad desert. They have come over, therefore, and are hastening up the chain to join the eager advance here so close to their hiding-place. Beyond a doubt watchful spies are already lurking among those heights to the west, striving to get close enough to peer into the rocky fortress and estimate the strength of the garrison. Great they well know it cannot be, for did not their keen eyes count nearly twenty chasing those hated brigands far down towards Sonora Pass, and of that number how many have returned?—only three. Did they not see the flurry

Charles King

and excitement when that sergeant was shot from ambush? Now, therefore, is the time to strike,—now while the main body is far away. Whatsoever booty there may be obtainable in that rocky canon 'tis well worth the attempt. And so from north to south the puff-balls of blue-white smoke go sailing upward through the pines, and it all means speed! speed!

At seven o'clock the little command has had coffee and a hearty breakfast. No lack of provender here in this hitherto undiscovered robbers' roost. Drummond, cool, confident, has had his men about him where none others could see or hear, has assigned them the stations which they are to take the instant of alarm, and has given them their instructions. Walsh it is who is now on lookout, and he is peering away down southward so intently that some comrade is prompted to call up to him in a low tone,—

"See anything?"

To which, without removing the glass from under his hat-brim, the Irish trooper merely shakes his head.

"Any more smokes?"

"Sorra a smoke have I seen at all."

"Well, then, what in blazes are you staring at?"

"How can I tell ye till I find out?" is the Hibernian reply, and this is enough to send the corporal on a climb. Drummond at the moment is again kneeling by Wing, who has but just awakened from a fitful sleep, Miss Harvey being the first to hear him stir and sigh. Ruth and her sister, too, seem about to withdraw, but Wing, whose voice is weak now, begs them to remain.

"Has anything been seen yet—back on the trail—of the Stoneman party?" he asks.

"No, sergeant," replies Drummond; "but remember that we can only see some six miles of the trail, after that it is lost in that tortuous ravine down which we rode on the chase. Walsh is up there on lookout, and I'll ask if he can see anything now;" and calling to one of the men, Drummond bids him inquire. All eagerly await the reply.

At last it comes,—

"No dust on the back track, sir, but something that looks like it far to the south. We think it may be some of our fellows coming back, but it is too faint and far to make it out yet."

The corporal is the speaker, his resonant voice contrasting strongly with the feeble accents of his immediate superior, the wounded sergeant.

"Then I have something that must be told you, lieutenant, something Miss Harvey already has an inkling of, for she has met and known my dear mother. If this pain continue to increase, and fever set in, I may be unable to tell it later. Some of the men thought I had enlisted under an alias, lieutenant, but they were wrong. Wing is my rightful name. My father was chief officer of the old 'Flying Cloud' in the days when American clipper ships beat the world. The gold fever seized him, though, and he quit sailing and went to mining in the early days of San Francisco, and there when I was a little boy of ten he died, leaving mother with not many thousand dollars to take care of herself and me. 'You will have your brother to help you' were words he spoke the last day of his life, and even then I noted how little comfort mother seemed to find in that fact. It was only a few months after father's death that Uncle Fred, from being an occasional visitor, came to living with us all the time, made his home there, though seldom within doors night or day. He was several years younger than mother. He was the youngest, it seems, of the family, 'the baby,' and had been petted and spoiled from earliest infancy. I soon found why he came. Mother was often in tears, Uncle Fred always begging or demanding money. The boys at school twitted me about my gambler uncle, though I've no doubt their fathers gambled as much as he. These were just before the early days of the great war that sprang up in '61 and that we boys out on the Pacific coast only vaguely understood. Sometimes Uncle Fred came home drunk and I could hear him threatening poor mother, and things went from bad to worse, and one night when I was just thirteen I was awakened from sound sleep by her scream. In an instant I flew to her room, catching up as I ran father's old bowie-knife that always hung by my door. In the dim light I saw her lying by the bedside, a man bending over and choking her. With all my strength I slashed at him just as he turned. I meant to kill, but the turn saved him. He sprang to his feet with an oath and cry and rushed to the wash-stand. I had laid Uncle Fred's cheek open from ear to chin.

"It was long before mother could check the flow of the blood. It sobered him, of course, and made him piteously weak. For days after that she nursed and cared for him, but forbade my entering the room. Men came to see him,— insisted on seeing him,—and she would send me to the bank for gold and pay their claims and bid them go. At last he was able to walk out with that awful slash on his thin white face. Once then he met and cursed me, but I did not mind, I had acted only to save mother. How could I suppose that her assailant was her own brother? Then finally with sobs and tears she told me the story, how he had been their mother's darling, how wild and reckless was his youth, how her mother's last thought seemed to be for him, and how on her knees she, my own mother, promised to take care of poor Freddie and shield him from every ill, and this promise she repeated to me, bidding me help her keep it and to conceal as far as I could her brother's misdeeds. For a few months things went a little better. Uncle Fred got a commission in a California regiment towards the close of the war and was sent down to Arizona. Then came more tears and trouble. I couldn't understand it all then, but I do now. Uncle Fred was gambling again, drawing on her for means to meet his losses. The old home went under the hammer, and we moved down to San Diego, where father had once invested and had left a little property. And then came the news that Uncle Fred had been dismissed, all on account of drink and gambling and misappropriation of funds. Miss Harvey knows all about this, lieutenant, for mother told her and had reason to. And next came forgery, and we were stranded. We heard that he had gone after that with a wagon-train to Texas. I got employment on a ranch, and then mother married again, married a man who had long befriended us and who could give her a comfortable home. She is now Mrs. Malcomb Bland, of San Francisco, and Mr. Bland offered to take me into his store, but I loved the open air and independence. Mr. Bland and Mr. Harvey had business relations, and when Uncle Fred was next heard from he was 'starving to death,' he said, 'actually dying.' He wrote to mother from Yuma. Mother wired me to go to him at once, and I did. He was considerably out at elbows, but in no desperate need yet. Just then Mr. Harvey offered him a good salary to take charge of his freight-train. We all knew how that must have been brought about, and I felt that it would only be a matter of time when he would rob his new employer. He did; was discharged, but Mr. Bland made the amount good, and the matter was hushed up. Then he drove stage awhile and then disappeared. Mother has written me time and again to find him or find out what has become of him, and I promised I would leave no stone unturned. Tell her I have kept my word. Tell her I found him.

But tell her for God's sake to think no more of him. Tell her not to strive to find him or to ask what he is or even where he is beyond that he has gone to Sonora."

"Lieutenant," said Patterson, suddenly appearing at the opening, "could you step here a moment?"

Drummond springs up.

"One moment, Mr. Drummond," whispers Wing, weakly; "I must say one word to you—alone."

"I'll return in a minute, sergeant. Let me see what Patterson wants."

Miss Harvey and Ruth have risen; the former is very pale and evidently trembling under some strong emotion. Once more she bends over him.

"Drink this, Mr. Wing, and now talk no more than you absolutely have to."

Then renewing the cooling bandage on his forehead, her hands seem to linger—surely her eyes do—as she rises once more to her feet.

Meantime the lieutenant has stepped out into the canon.

"What is it, Patterson? quick!"

"That was some of our fellows, sir, a squad of four; but they turned all of a sudden and galloped back out of sight. It looks to me as though they were attacked."

"How far away were they? How many miles down the desert?"

"Oh, at least six or eight miles down, sir; down beyond where you met them yesterday."

"How about our trail? Anybody in sight there?"

"Nobody, sir, not even a thing, not even a whiff of dust."

"Very well. Keep on the alert. It's good to know that all the Apaches are not around us yet. Neither bullet nor arrow can get down here so long as we man the rocks above. I'll be out in a moment."

Then once more he kneels by Wing.

"Lieutenant, did you ever see a girl behave with greater bravery? Do you know what she has undergone?—Miss Harvey, I mean?"

"Both are behaving like heroines, Wing, and I think I am beginning to see through this plot at last."

"Never let mother know it,—promise me, sir,—but when Harvey discharged him—my uncle, I mean—he swore he'd be revenged on the old man, and 'twas he—"

"The double-dyed villain! I know, I understand now, Wing; you needn't tell me. He has been in the pay of the Morales gang for months. He enlisted so as to learn all the movements of officers and scouting-parties. He enlisted under his benefactor's name. He has forged that, too, in all probability, and then, deserting, it was he who sought to carry away these precious girls, and he came within an ace of succeeding. By the Eternal, but there will be a day of reckoning for him if ever 'C' troop runs foul of him again! No wonder you couldn't sleep, poor fellow, for thinking of that mother. This caps the climax of his scoundrelism. Where,—when did you see him last?—since he enlisted?"

But now Wing's face is again averted. He is covering it with his arms.

"Wing, answer me!" exclaims Drummond, springing suddenly to his feet. "By heaven, I demand to know!" Then down on his knees he goes again, seizing and striving to pull away the nearest arm. "You need not try, you cannot conceal it now. I see it all,—all. Miss Harvey," he cries, looking up into the face of the trembling girl, who has hastened in at sound of the excitement in his voice,—"Miss Harvey, think of it; 'twas no Apache who shot him, 'twas a worse savage,—his own uncle."

"Promise me mother shall not know," pleads poor Wing, striving to rise upon his elbow, striving to restrain the lieutenant, who again has started to his feet. "Promise me, Miss Fanny; you know how she loved him, how she plead with you."

"I promise you this, Wing," says Drummond, through his clinching teeth, "that there'll be no time for prayer if ever we set eyes on him again; there'll be no mercy."

"You can't let your men kill him in cold blood, lieutenant. I could not shoot him."

"No, but, by the God of heaven, I could!"

And now as Wing, exhausted, sinks back to his couch his head is caught on Fanny Harvey's arm and next is pillowed in her lap.

"Hush!" she murmurs, bending down over him as mother might over sleeping child. "Hush! you must not speak again. I know how her heart is bound up in you, and I'm to play mother to you now."

And as Drummond, tingling all over with wrath and excitement, stands spellbound for the moment, a light step comes to his side, a little hand is laid on the bandaged arm, and Ruth Harvey's pretty face, two big tears trickling down her cheeks, is looking up in his.

"You, too, will be ill, Mr. Drummond. Oh, why can't you go and lie down and rest? What will we do if both of you are down at once with fever?"

She is younger by over two years than her brave sister. Tall though she has grown, Ruth is but a child, and now in all her excitement and anxiety, worn out with the long strain, she begins to cry. She strives to hide it, strives to control the weakness, and, failing in both, strives to turn away. All to no purpose. An arm in a sling is of little avail at such a moment. Whirling quickly about, Drummond brings his other into action. Before the weeping little maid is well aware what is happening her waist is encircled by the strong arm in the dark-blue sleeve, and how can she see that she is drawn to his breast, since now her face is buried in both her hands and those hands in the flannel of his hunting-shirt,—just as high as his heart? Small wonder is it that Corporal Costigan, hurrying in at the mouth of the cave, stops short at sight of this picturesque *partie carree*. Any other time he would have sense enough to face about and tiptoe whence he came, but now there's no room left for sentiment. *Tableaux-vivants* are lovely in their way, even in a cave lighted dimly by a hurricane-lamp, but sterner scenes are on the curtain. Drummond's voice is murmuring soothing, yes, caressing words to his sobbing captive. Drummond's bearded lips, unrebuked, are actually pressing a kiss upon that childish brow when Costigan, with a preliminary clearing of his throat that sounds like a landslide and makes the rock walls ring again, startles Ruth from her blissful woe and brings Drummond leaping to the mouth of the cave.

"Lieutenant, there's something coming out over our trail."

"Thank God!" sighs Wing, as he raises his eyes to those of his fair nurse. "Thank God! for your sakes!"

"Thank God, Ruth!" cries Fanny, extending one hand to her sister while the other is unaccountably detained. "Thank God! it's father and the Stoneman party and Doctor Gray."

And Ruth, throwing herself upon her knees by her sister's side, buries her head upon her shoulder and sobs anew for very joy.

And then comes sudden start. All in an instant there rings, echoing down the canon, the sharp, spiteful crack of rifles, answered by shrieks of terror from the cave where lie the Moreno women, and by other shots out along the range. Three faces blanch with sudden fear, though Wing looks instantly up to say,—

"They can't harm you, and our men will be here in less than no time."

Out in the gorge men are springing to their feet and seizing their ready arms; horses are snorting and stamping; mules braying in wild terror. Two of the ambulance mules, breaking loose from their fastenings, come charging down the resounding rock, nearly annihilating Moreno, who, bound and helpless, praying and cursing by turns, has rolled himself out of his nook and lies squarely in the way of everything and everybody. But above all the clamor, the ring of carbine, the hiss and spat of lead flattening upon the rocks, Drummond's voice is heard clear and commanding, serene and confident.

"Every man to his post now. Remember your orders."

Gazing out into the canon with dilated eyes, Ruth sees him nimbly clamber up the opposite side towards the point where Walsh is kneeling behind a rock,—Walsh with his Irish mug expanded in a grin of delight, the smoke just drifting from the muzzle of his carbine as he points with his left hand somewhere out along the cliffs. She sees her soldier boy, crouching low, draw himself to Walsh's side, sees him glancing eagerly over the rocks, then signalling to some one on their own side, pointing here and there along the wooded slope beyond her vision; sees him now, with fierce light in his eyes, suddenly clutch Walsh's sleeve and nod towards some invisible object to the south; sees Walsh toss the butt of his carbine to the shoulder and with quick aim send a bullet driving thither; sees Drummond take the field-glass and, resting it on the eastward ledge, gaze long and fixedly out over the eastward way; sees him start, draw back the glass, wipe the lenses with his silken kerchief, then peer again; sees him drop them with a gesture almost tragic, but she cannot hear the moan that rises to his lips.

"My God! those are Apaches, too."

XI

Ten o'clock on a blazing Arizona morning. The hot sun is
pouring down upon the jagged front of a range of heights
where occasional clumps of pine and cedar, scrub oak and
juniper, seemed the only vegetable products hardy enough to
withstand the alternations of intense heat by day and
moderate cold by night, or to find sufficient sustenance to
eke out a living on so barren a soil. Out to the eastward,
stretching away to an opposite range, lies a sandy desert
dotted at wide intervals with little black bunches of "scrub
mezquite" and blessed with only one redeeming patch of
foliage, the copse of willows and cottonwood here at the
mouth of a rock-ribbed defile where a little brook, rising
heaven knows how or where among the heights to the west,
comes frothing and tumbling down through the windings of
the gorge only to bury itself in the burning sands beyond the
shade. So narrow and tortuous is the canon, so precipitous its
sides, as to prove conclusively that by no slow process, but
by some sudden spasm of nature, was it rent in the face of
the range. And here in its depths, just around one of the
sharpest bends, honey-combed out of the solid rock are half a
dozen deep lateral fissures and caves where the sunbeams
never penetrate, where the air is reasonably cool and still,
where on this scorching May morning, far away from home
and relatives, two young girls are sheltered by the natural
roofs and walls against the fiery sunshine and by a little band

of resolute men against the fury of the Apaches.

Down in the roomiest of the caves Fanny and Ruth Harvey are listening in dread anxiety to the sounds of savage warfare echoing from crag to crag along the range, while every moment or two the elder turns to moisten the cloth she holds to a wounded trooper's burning, tossing head. Sergeant Wing is fevered indeed by this time, raging with misery at thought of his helplessness and the scant numbers of the defence. It is a bitter pill for the soldier to swallow, this of lying in hospital when every man is needed at the front. At nine o'clock this morning a veteran Indian fighter, crouching in his sheltered lookout above the caves and scanning with practised eye the frowning front of the range, declared that not an Apache was to be seen or heard within rifle-shot, yet was in no wise surprised when, a few minutes later, as he happened to show his head above the rocky parapet, there came zipping a dozen bullets about his ears and the cliffs fairly crackled with the sudden flash of rifles hidden up to that instant on every side. Indians who can creep upon wagon-train or emigrant camp in the midst of an open and unsheltered plain find absolutely no difficulty in surrounding unsuspected and unseen a bivouac in the mountains. Inexperienced officers or men would have been picked off long before the opening of the general attack, but the Apaches themselves are the first to know that they have veteran troopers to deal with, for up to this moment only one has shown himself at all. At five minutes after nine o'clock Lieutenant Drummond, glancing exultingly around upon his little band of fighters, had blessed the foresight of Pasqual Morales and his gang that they had so thoroughly fortified their lair against sudden assault. Three on the southern, two on the northern brink of the gorge and behind impenetrable shelter, and two more in reserve in the canon, his puny garrison was in position and had replied with such spirit and promptitude to the Apache attack that only at rare intervals

Charles King

now is a shot necessary, except when for the purpose of drawing the enemy and locating his position a hat is poked up on the muzzle of a carbine. The assailants' fire, too, is still, but that, as Drummond's men well know, means only "look out for other devilment."

Out on the eastward desert, still far over towards the other side, a little party of Apaches is hurrying to join the fray. Two are riding. Where got they their horses? The others—over half a dozen—come along at their tireless jog-trot. It was this party that, seen but dimly at first, gave rise to such ebullition of joy among the defenders and defended. It was this party that, closely scanned through his field-glass, occasioned Lieutenant Drummond's moan of distress. With all his heart he had been hoping for the speedy coming of relief over that very trail,—had counted on its reaching him during the day. He was sure it could be nothing else when the corporal reported something in sight, and so when he discovered the approaching party to be Apaches no words could describe the measure of his disappointment and dismay. Not for himself and his men; they were old hands and had a fine position to defend. His thoughts are all for those in whose behalf he has already made such gallant fight and for poor Wing, whose feeble moaning every now and then reaches his ear.

At ten o'clock he is able through his glasses to distinctly make out the number and character of the coming party. Nine Apaches, all warriors, but one of them apparently wounded or disabled, for they have to support him on the horse, and this it is that hampers their advance and makes it slower. They are heading for the oasis at the mouth of the canon. There they will leave their horses and their wounded, and then come creeping up the winding gorge or crouching among the bowlders from the east to join in the attack on the hated pale-face. Drummond can have no doubt of that. New dispositions are necessary.

"Stay where you are!" he shouts to his men. "You take charge up here, Costigan; I want to post a man or two below at the bend." And down he goes, sliding and scrambling until he reaches the edge of the brook. Moreno, squatted against a rock, glances up at him appealingly.

"Senor Teniente, I pray you unloose me and let me help. The Apache is our common enemy," he pleads.

An idea comes to Drummond. Wing's carbine can be utilized. He can post Moreno down the gorge at the second bend to command that approach and put little McGuffey, the recruit, at the next bend to command Moreno and send a bullet through him if he shirk or swerve.

"I declare, I believe I will, you old scoundrel," he says. "Here, McGuffey, untie this fellow. I've got to look around a minute."

Into the depth of the fissure where Moreno's women are praying and rocking he peers a moment. One of the wounded bandits is now past praying for. The other, painfully shot but plucky, begs to be given a chance to fight for his life.

"You are too badly hurt now. We couldn't get you up there," is the answer.

"Well, then, put me on with Moreno, wherever you're going to assign him. Surely if you can trust a Greaser you can a white man. I'm only fit to hang, perhaps, but damn me if I want to lie here when there's an Indian fight going on."

And so he, too, is unloosed and lifted to his feet. Leaning on McGuffey's shoulder and supported by his arm, the pale-faced stranger, preceded by Moreno, who goes limping and swearing *sotto voce* down the rocky way, is led a hundred yards along the canon where it makes a second bend. Here they can see nearly one hundred and fifty more ahead of them, and here some loose bowlders are hurriedly shoved or rolled to form a rifle-pit, and these volunteer allies are placed in position.

"We cover the approaches above so that they can't sneak up and heave rocks down upon you. All you've got to do now is to plug every Apache that shows his nose around that bend below," says Drummond. "McGuffey, you take post at the point behind. Watch the overhanging cliffs and support as best you can." And "Little Mack," as the men call him, gets further instructions as he takes his position, instructions which would give small comfort to Moreno could he only hear them. Then back goes the lieutenant to where Wing is lying, Miss Harvey bending anxiously over him, her beautiful eyes filling with tears at sight of Drummond's brave but haggard young face. Ruth is crouching by her sister's side, but rises quickly as Drummond enters, her fears lessening, her hopes gaining.

"Any news? Anything in sight—of ours?" is Miss Harvey's eager query.

"Not yet, but they're bound to be along almost any minute now. Some Apaches whom I could see coming across from the east have a wounded man with them. It makes me hope our fellows have met and fought them and are following close on their trail. How's Wing?"

She can only shake her head.

"He seems delirious every now and then; perhaps only because of so much mental excitement and suffering. He is dozing now."

"Gallant fellow! What would we have done without him? I only wish we had more like him. Think how all my detachment has become scattered. If we had them here now I could push out and drive the Indians to the rocks and far beyond all possibility of annoying you with their racket. Of course you are safe from their missiles down here."

"Yes, *we* are; but you and your soldiers, Mr. Drummond! Every shot made me fear you were hit," cries poor little Ruth, her eyes filling, her lips quivering. Then, just as Drummond is holding forth a hand, perhaps it is an arm, too, she points up to the rock above where Walsh is evidently exercised about something. He has dropped his gun, picked up the glasses, and is gazing down the range to the south.

"Perhaps he sees some of our fellows coming for good this time. Four of them tried it awhile ago, but were probably attacked some miles below here and fell back on the main body. They'll be along before a great while, and won't it be glorious if they bring back the safe and all?" He says this by way of keeping up their spirits, then, once more wearily, but full of pluck and purpose, he climbs the rugged path and creeps to Walsh's side.

"Is it any of our men you see?" he whispers.

"Divil a wan, sir! it's more of thim infernal Apaches."

Drummond takes the glass and studies the dim and distant group with the utmost care. Apaches beyond doubt, a dozen, and coming this way, and these, too, have a couple of horses. Can they have overpowered his men, ambushed and murdered them, then secured their mounts? Is the whole Chiricahua tribe, reinforced by a swarm from the Sierra

Blanca, concentrating on him now? The silence about him is ominous. Not an Indian has shown along the range for half an hour, and now these fellows to the east are close to the copse. In less than twenty minutes there will be five times his puny force around him. Is there no hope of rescue?

Once more he turns to the east, across the shimmering glare of that parched and tawny plain, and strains his eyes in vain effort to catch sight of the longed-for column issuing from the opposite valley, but it is hopeless. The hot sun beats down upon his bruised and aching head and sears his bloodshot eyes. He raises his hand in mute appeal to heaven, and at the instant there is a flash, a sharp report not thirty yards away, an angry spat as the leaden missile strikes the shelving top of his parapet and goes humming across the gorge, a stifled shriek from Ruth looking fearfully up from below, an Irish oath from Walsh as he whirls about to answer the shot, and Drummond can barely repress a little gasp.

"Narrow squeak that, Walsh! That devil has crawled close up on us. Can you see him?"

"Begad, sir, I can see nothing at all but rocks, rocks, rocks. How can a man fight anyway agin' human beings that crawl like snakes?"

Zip! Another shot close at hand, too, and from another unseen foe. The first came from somewhere among the bowlders down to the southeast, and this second whizzed from across the canon. A little puff of blue smoke is floating up from among the rocks fifty yards or so to the north of the narrow slit.

Crouching lower, Drummond calls across to Costigan, posted as the easternmost of the two men on the opposite side,—

"That fellow is nearest you, corporal; can you see nothing of him?"

"Nothing, sir; I was looking that way, too, when he fired. Not even the muzzle of his gun showed."

This is serious business. If one Indian or two can find it so easy to creep around them and, armed only with their old muzzle-loading guns, send frequent shots that reach the besieged "in reverse," what can be hoped when the whole band gathers and every rock on every side shelters a hostile Apache? From the first Drummond has feared that however effective might be these defences against the open attack of white men, they are ill adapted to protect the defenders against the fire of Indians who can climb like squirrels or crawl or squirm through any chink or crevice like so many snakes.

Another shot! Another bullet flattens itself on the rock close to his right shoulder and then drops into the dust by his knee. It comes from farther up the cliff,—perhaps two hundred yards away among those stunted cedars,—but shudderingly close. Costigan and the other men glance anxiously over their shoulders at the point where their young commander and Walsh are crouching. They are not yet subjected to a fire from the rear, these others. The lookout, the signal-station, as it might be called, is the highest point and most exposed about the position.

"For God's sake, lieutenant," cries the corporal, "don't stay there. They've got your range on two sides anyhow. Come out of it. You and Walsh can slip down as we open fire. We'll just let drive in every direction until you are safe below."

Drummond hesitates. He sees a half-pleading look in Walsh's

honest face. The Irishman would willingly tackle the whole tribe in open fight, but what he doesn't like is the idea of being potted like a caged tiger, never knowing whence came the shot that laid him low. Then the lieutenant peers about him. Yes, it is exposed to fire from a point in the cliffs to the west, and there are rocks over there to the north that seem to command it; but if abandoned there will be no way of preventing a bold advance on part of the Apaches up the rugged eastward slope. It would then stand between the defenders and the assailants, giving to the latter incalculable advantage. Hold it he must for a few minutes at least, until, recalling McGuffey, he can set him and one or two others to work piling up a rock barricade in front of the cave. Then if driven out and no longer able to stand the Indians off, they can retire into the caves themselves, hide their precious charges in the farthest depths, and then, like Buford at Gettysburg, "fight like the devil" till rescue come.

"No, down with you, Costigan," he answers. "Get McGuffey and Fritz; block up the front of the cave with rocks; move in those Moreno women; carry Sergeant Wing back to the farther cave,—Miss Harvey will show you where. Stand fast the rest of you. Don't let an Indian close in on us."

"Look, lieut'nant," whispers Walsh; "they're coming up down beyant you there."

And, peeping through a narrow slit left in his parapet, Drummond can just see bobbing among the bowlders far down towards the willow copse two or three Apache crests,—Apache unmistakably, because of the dirty-white turban-like bandages about the matted black locks. At that distance they advance with comparative security. It is when they come closer to the defenders that they will be lost to view.

Obedient to his orders, Costigan slips out of his shelter and "takes a sneak" for the edge of the cliff. In an instant, from half a dozen points above, below, and on both sides, there come the flash and crack of rifles. The dust is kicked up under his nimble feet, but he reaches unharmed the cleft in which some rude steps have been hacked, and goes, half sliding, half scraping, down into the cooler depths below.

"Mother of Moses!" he groans, "but we'll never get the lieut'nant out alive. Shure they're all around him now."

Then bounding down the gorge he finds McGuffey kneeling at the point.

"They're coming, Barney," whispers the boy, all eager and tremulous with excitement, and pointing down between the vertical walls. "Look!" he says.

Gazing ahead to the next bend, Costigan can see Moreno and his Yankee *compadre* crouching behind their shelter, their carbines levelled, their attitude betokening intense excitement and suspense. It is evident the enemy are within view.

"I'll have one shot at 'em, bedad, to pay for the dozen their brother blackguards let drive at me," mutters Costigan. "Come on, you; it's but a step." And, forgetful for the moment of his orders in his eagerness for fight, the Irishman runs down the canon, leaps the swirling brook just as he reaches the point, and, obedient to the warning hand held out by their bandit ally, drops on his knees at the bend, McGuffey close at his heels. Off go their hats. Those broad brims would catch an Indian eye even in that gloom.

"How many are there coming?" he whispers.

Moreno puts his finger on his lips, then throws out his hand, four fingers extended.

"One apiece then, be jabers! Now, Little Mac, you're to take the second from the right,—their right, I mean,—and doan't you miss him or I'll break every bone in your skin."

"Hist!"

Down they go upon their faces, then, Indian-like, they crawl a few feet farther where there is a little ledge. The canon widens below; the light is stronger there, and, bending double, throwing quick glances at one another, then from sheer force of Indian habit shading their eyes with their brown hands as they peer to the front; exchanging noiseless signals; creeping like cats from rock to rock; leaping without faintest sound of the moccasined foot across the bubbling waters, four swarthy scamps are coming stealthily on. Two others are just appearing around the next bend beyond.

"Ready, boys? They're near enough now. Cover the two leaders! Drop the first two anyhow!"

Breathless silence, thumping hearts one instant longer, then the chasm bellows with the loud reports. The four guns are fired almost as one. One half-naked wretch leaps high in air and falls, face downward, dead as a nail. Another whirls about, bounds a few yards along the brook-side, and then goes splashing into a shallow pool, where he lies writhing. The two farthest down the canon have slipped back behind the rocky shoulder. The other two, close at hand, have rolled behind the nearest shelter and thence send harmless bullets whizzing overhead. Costigan lets drive a wild Irish yell of triumph and delight.

"Now, then, run for it, boy. Well done, you two, if ye are blackguards," he calls to Moreno and his mate. "They won't disturb ye again for ten minutes anyhow. Hold your post, though, till we call you back. We're going to block the mouth of the cave."

Twenty minutes later and, working like beavers, Costigan and his two men have lugged rocks, logs, bales of blankets, everything, anything that can stop a bullet, and the entrance to the cave is being stoutly barricaded. Patterson, who was sorely exposed at his post and ordered down by Lieutenant Drummond, is aiding in the work. Wing has been carefully borne into the back cave, whither, too, the wailing, quaking Moreno women are herded and bidden to hold their peace. There, too, Fanny and Ruth, silent, pallid perhaps, but making no moan, are now kneeling by their patient. Costigan runs in with two buckets he has filled with water and "Little Mac" follows with half a dozen dripping canteens. More rocks are being lifted on the barricade, convenient apertures being left through which to fire, and Costigan, feverishly eager, is making every exertion, for any minute may be the last with those plucky fellows battling there aloft. The air rings with the shots of the encircling Apaches and with the loud report of the cavalry carbine answering the hidden foe. Twice has Costigan implored the lieutenant to come down anyhow, so long as his crippled condition prevents his firing a gun, but Drummond pokes his bandaged head one instant over the edge to shout something to the effect that he is "on deck" until he has seen the last man down, and Costigan knows it is useless to argue. At last the barricade is ready. Walsh, peering grimly around, just the top of his head showing over the parapet, begs for one shot and shouts his Hibernian challenge to the Apache nation to come forth and show itself. Drummond picks up the glasses for one final look down the desert and across the valley in search of friends who surely should be coming, cautiously places the "binocular" on the inner edge of the top of his shelving rock, then raises his head to the level.

"Fur the love o' God, loot'n'nt, don't sit so high up!" implores Walsh. "They're sure to spot—Oh, Christ!" And down goes the poor faithful fellow, the blood welling from a deep gash along the temple. He lies senseless at his commander's feet.

For a moment the air seems alive with humming missiles and shrill with yells from on every side. In their triumph three or four savage foes have leaped up from behind their sheltering rocks, and one of them pays the penalty,—a vengeful carbine from across the canon stretches the lithe, slender, dusky form lifeless among the rocks, with the dirty white of his breech-clout turning crimson in the noonday glare. Up from the cave, cat-like, Patterson and "Little Mac" come climbing the narrow trail. Between them they drag Walsh's senseless body to the edge, and then, somehow, despite hissing, spattering lead, they bear him safely down and carry him within the cave.

"Now call in Moreno and help his partner back!" shouts Drummond, and Costigan goes at speed to carry out the order. A few minutes of intense excitement and suspense, then Moreno is seen limping around the point. Behind him Costigan is slowly helping their brigand friend. A few more shots come singing overhead. A moment more and the watchful Indians will come charging up the now unguarded canon and crowning both banks.

"Now, lads, give 'em two or three shots apiece to make them hug their cover. Then down for the caves, every man of you," is the order.

For a moment the Indian fire is silenced in the rapid fusillade that follows. Sharp and quick the carbines are barking their challenge, and whenever a puff of powder-smoke has marked the probable lurking-place of an Apache, thither hiss the searching bullets warning him to keep down. Then

Costigan comes climbing to the lookout.

"Let us help you, lieut'nant; now's your time, sir, while they're firing."

But Drummond shakes his head. He wants to be the last man down.

"Don't hang on here, sir. Come now. Sure the others can get down from where they are easy enough, but you can't except when they're firing. Please come, sir," and Costigan in his eagerness scrambles to the lieutenant's side and lays a broad, red hand on his shoulder. The men have fired more than the designated number of shots and now are looking anxiously towards their commander. They do not wish to move until he does.

"Give 'em another whack all around, fellers," shouts Costigan, "while I help the loot'n'nt down;" and so, with a laugh, Drummond gives it up, and after one last wistful glance out over the desert, turns to pick up the binocular, when it is struck, smashed, and sent clattering down into the canon by a shot fired not twenty yards away.

"Fur God's sake come quick, sir!" gasps Costigan. Then, desperate at his loved young leader's delay, the Irishman throws a brawny arm about him and fairly drags him to the end of the steep. Then down they go, Costigan leading and holding up one hand to sustain Drummond in case of accident. Down, hand under hand, to the accompaniment of cracking rifles and answering carbines, while every other second the bullets come "spat" upon the rocky sides, close and closer, until, panting, almost breathless, Costigan reaches the solid bottom of the gorge and swings Drummond to his feet beside him. Seeing their leader safely down, the men, with one defiant shot and cheer, scurry to the edge of the canon, and come slipping and sliding to join their comrades. At the mouth of the cave Costigan strives to push Drummond in through the narrow aperture left for their admission, but miscalculates his commander's idea of the proprieties. Like gallant Craven at Mobile Bay, Drummond will seek no safety until his men are cared for. "After you, pilot," the chivalric sailor's last word as the green waters engulfed his sinking ship, finds its cavalry echo in Drummond's "After you, corporal," in this far-away canon in desert Arizona. The men have scrambled through the gap, then Costigan, with reluctant backward glance, is hurried in just as a flash of flame and smoke leaps downward from the crest and the foremost Apache sends a hurried, ill-aimed shot at the last man left. Before another shot can follow, Drummond's arm is seized by muscular hands and he is dragged within the gap. Two or three huge stones are rolled into place, and in an instant through the ragged loop-holes the black muzzles of half a dozen carbines are thrusting, and Costigan shouts exultingly, "Now, you black-legged blackguards, come on if ye dare!"

But no Apache is fool enough to attack a strong position. Keeping well under cover, the Indians soon line the crest and begin sending down a rain of better-aimed bullets at the loop-holes, and every minute the flattened lead comes zipping through. One of these fearful missiles tears its way through Costigan's sleeve and, striking poor old Moreno in the groin, stretches him groaning upon the floor. A glance shows that the wound is mortal, and, despite his crimes, the men who bear him, moaning, in to the farther cave are moved to sudden sympathy as his hapless wife and child prostrate themselves beside his rocky bier. Drummond can afford to lose no more, and orders the lower half of each hole to be stopped with blankets, blouses, shirts, anything that will block a shot, and then for an hour the fire of the besiegers is harmless, and no longer can the besieged catch even an occasional glimpse of them. At noon their fire has ceased entirely and, even when breathing a sigh of relief, the men look into one another's faces questioningly. How long can this last? How hot, how close the air in the cave is growing!

Drummond has gone for a moment into the inner chamber, where Moreno is now breathing his last, to inquire for Wing and to speak a word of cheer to his fair and devoted nurses. Not one murmur of complaint or dread has fallen from their lips, though they know their father to have ridden on perilous quest and into possible ambush; though they know their brother to be lying at the ruined ranch, perhaps seriously wounded; though their own fate may be capture, with indescribable suffering, shame, and death. Fanny Harvey has behaved like a heroine, as the two troopers remarked, and Ruth has done her best to follow her sister's lead. Yet they, too, now realize how close and stifling the heavy atmosphere is growing. Is it to be black hole of Calcutta over again? Even as he takes her hand in his Drummond reads the dread in Ruth's tearless face. Even as he holds it and whispers words of hope and comfort there is a heavy, continuous, crashing sound at the mouth of the cave, just in front of the rock barricade, and he springs back to learn the cause.

"They're heaving down logs and brushwood, sir," whispers Costigan. "They mean to roast us out if they can't do anything else."

More thunder and crash; more heaping up of resinous logs from the cliffs above them. Some of the men beg to be allowed to push out and die fighting, but Drummond sternly refuses. "At the worst," he says, "we can retire into the back cave; we have abundant water there. The air will last several hours yet, and I tell you help will come,—*must* come, before the day is much older."

Two o'clock. Hissing flames and scorching heat block the cavern entrance. The rocky barrier grows hotter and hotter; the air within denser and more stifling. The water in the canteens and pails is no longer cool. It is hardly even cooling. The few men who remain with Drummond in the front of the cave are lying full length upon the floor. The pain in Drummond's battered head has become intense: it is almost maddening. Wing is moaning and unconscious. Walsh is incoherent and raving. All are panting and well-nigh exhausted. The front of the cave is like an oven. Overcome by the heat, one or two of the men are edging towards the inner cave, but Drummond orders them back. To the very last the lives of those fair girls must be protected and cherished. In silence, almost in desperation, the men obey, and lie down again, face downward, their heads at the rear wall of the cave.

And then Costigan comes crawling to the lieutenant's side,—

"Have you heard any more logs thrown down lately, sir?"

"No, corporal. I have heard nothing."

"They were yellin' and shootin' out there in the gulch half an hour ago. Have ye heard no more of it, sir?"

"No; no sound but the flames."

"Glory be to God, thin! D'ye know what it manes, sir?"

"I know what I hope," is Drummond's faint answer. "Our fellows are close at hand, for the Indians are clearing out."

"Close at hand, is it?" cries Costigan, in wild excitement, leaping to his feet. "Listen, sir! Listen, all of ye's! D'ye hear that?—and that? And *there* now! Oh, Holy Mother of God!

isn't that music? Thim's the thrumpets of 'K' throop!"

Ay. Out along the crests of the winding canon the rifles are ringing again. The cheers of troopers, bounding like goats up the rocky sides, are answered by clatter of hoof and snort of excited steeds in the rocky depths below. "Here we are, lads! Dismount! Lively now!" a well-known voice is ordering, and Costigan fairly screams in ecstasy of joy, "Tear away the fire, captain, an' then we'll heave over the rocks."

Stalwart forms, brawny arms, are already at the work. The wagon-tongues are prying under the heavy, hissing, sputtering logs. Daring hands scatter the embers. Buckets of water are dashed over the live coals. "Up wid ye now, boys!" shouts Costigan. "Heave over thim rocks!" Down with a crash goes the barricade. A cloud of steam rushes into the cave. A dozen sturdy troopers come leaping in, lifting from the ground the helpless and bearing them to the blessed coolness of the outer air, and the last thing Jim Drummond sees—ere he swoons away—is the pale, senseless face of little Ruth close to his at the water's brink; her father, with Fanny clinging about his neck, kneeling by her side, his eyes uplifted in thanks to the God who even through such peril and distress has restored his loved ones, unharmed, unstained, to his rejoicing heart.

Charles King

XII

It is a sultry day, early in July, and the sun is going westward through a fleet of white, wind-driven clouds that send a host of deep shadows sweeping and chasing over the wide prairie. Northwards the view is limited by a low range of bluffs, destitute of tree or foliage, but covered thickly with the summer growth of bunch-grass. Southward, three miles away at least, though it seems much less, a similar range, pierced here and there with deep ravines, frames the picture on that side. Midway between the two ridges and fringed with clumps of cottonwood and willow, a languid stream flows silently eastward and is lost, with the valley, in the dim distance. Out to the west in long, gradual curve the southward range veers around and spans the horizon. Midway across this monotone of landscape, cutting the stream at right angles, a hard prairie road comes twisting and turning out of one of the southern ravines and, after long, gradual dip to the ford among the cottonwoods, emerges from their leafy shade and goes winding away until lost among the "breaks" to the north. It is one of the routes to the Black Hills of Dakota,—the wagon road from the Union Pacific at Sidney by way of old Fort Robinson, Nebraska, where a big garrison of some fourteen companies of cavalry and infantry keep watch and ward over the Sioux Nation, which, one year previous, was in the midst of the maddest, most successful, war it ever waged against the white man.

That was the Centennial year—'76. This is another eventful year for the cavalry,—'77; for before the close of the summer even the troops so far to the southeast are destined to be summoned to the chase and capture of wary old Chief Joseph,—the greatest Indian general ever reared upon the Pacific slope,—and even now, on this July day, here are cavalrymen at their accustomed task, and though it is five years since we saw them under the heat and glare of the Arizona sun, there are familiar faces among these that greet us.

All along under the cottonwoods below the crossing the bivouac extends. Long before sunrise these hardy fellows were in saddle and, in long column, have come marching down from the north,—four strong troops,—a typical battalion of regular cavalry as they looked and rode in those stirring days that brought about the subjugation of the Sioux. Out on the prairie the four herds of the four different troops are quietly grazing, each herd watched by its trio of alert, though often apparently dozing, guards. One troop is made up entirely of black horses, another of sorrels,—two are of bays. Another herd is grazing close to the stream,—the mules of the wagon-train, and the white tops of these cumbrous vehicles are dotting the left bank of the winding water for two or three hundred yards. Cook-fires are smouldering in little pits dug in the yielding soil, but the cooking is over for the present; the men have had their substantial dinner and are now smoking or sleeping or chatting in groups in the shade,—all but a squad of a dozen, commanded by a grizzled veteran on whose worn blouse the chevrons of a first sergeant are stitched. Booted and spurred, with carbines slung and saddles packed, these sun-tanned fellows are standing or sitting at ease, holding the reins of their sleepy chargers and waiting apparently for the passengers who are to start in the stout-built "Concord" drawn by four sleek, strong-looking mules, now standing in

Charles King

the shade near the canvas homestead of the commanding officer.

Presently two soldiers following a young man in civilian dress come forward lugging a little green painted iron safe, and this, with a swing and a thud, they deposit in the wagon.

"You've seen that before, sergeant," laughs the civilian.

"I have, begad, an' when it had a heap more green inside an' less outside than it has now. Faith, I never expected to see it again, nor the paymaster either. We were both bored through and through. 'Twas our good habits that saved us. Sure your predecessor was a game fighter, Mr. Barnes, if he *was* a tenderfoot."

"Yes, the major often tells me he wishes he had him back, and me in the place he has instead of the one he had," answers the clerk, whimsically. "Does he know you're to command the escort in? You got him into such a scrape then that he's never tired of telling of it."

"Then he may feel gratified at the honor I am doing him now. Sure it's beneath the dignity of a first sergeant to command a squad like this except on extraordinary occasion, and it's to take the taste of the last time out of his mouth I volunteered to escort the major now. 'Twas a strong taste to last five years, though my reminder will go with me many a year longer. Here they come now."

As the sergeant speaks a little group of officers issues from the battalion commander's tent. Foremost among them, in loose flapping raiment and broad-brimmed hat and green goggles, the rotund and portly shape of Major Plummer, the paymaster.

"Well, old man," says the cavalry leader, "you can hardly get into a scrape 'twixt here and Sidney. We've seen you through all right so far; now we'll go on about our scouting. Your old friend Feeny asked permission to see you safely to the railway."

"What, Feeny? and a first sergeant too? I'm honored, indeed! Well, sergeant," he adds, catching sight of the grizzled red face under the old scouting hat, "I'll promise to let you run the machine this time and not interfere, no matter what stories come to us of beauty in distress. All ready?"

"All ready, sir, if the major is."

"He wasn't that civil to me in Arizona," laughs the pay-master, as he turns to shake hands with the officers about him.

"You see you were new to the business then," explains a tall captain; "Feeny considers you a war veteran now, after your experience at Moreno's. We all had to serve our apprenticeship as suckling lieutenants before he would show us anything but a semblance of respect. Good-by, major; good luck to you."

"Good-by all. Good-by, Drummond. Good-by, Wing.— Here! I must shake hands with you two again." And shake he does; then is slowly "boosted" into his wagon, where, as the whip cracks and the mules plunge at their collars and tilt him backward, the major's jolly red face beams on all around, and he waves his broad-brimmed hat in exuberant cordiality as they rattle away.

The group of officers presently disperses, two tall lieutenants strolling off together and throwing themselves under the spreading branches of a big cottonwood. One of them, darker and somewhat heavier built now, but muscular, active, powerful, is Drummond; the other, a younger man by a brace of years, tall, blue-eyed, blonde-bearded, wearing on his scouting-blouse the straps of a second lieutenant, is our old friend Wing, and Wing does not hesitate in presence of his senior officer—such is the bond of friendship between them—to draw from his breast-pocket a letter just received that day when the courier met them at the crossing of the Dry Fork, and to lose himself in its contents.

"All well with the madam and the kid?" queries Drummond, after the manner of the frontier, when at last Wing folds and replaces his letter, a happy light in his brave blue eyes.

"All well; Paquita says that Harvey has captured the entire household, and that Grandpa Harvey is his abject slave. There isn't anything in Chicago too good for that two-year-old. They've had them photo'd together,—the kid on his grandfather's shoulder."

"Aren't you afraid his Arizona uncle will be jealous for his own boy's sake?" laughs Drummond.

"I don't believe Ned would begrudge Fanny anything the old man might feel for her or for hers. He is generosity itself towards his sisters, and surely I could never have found a warmer friend—out of the army. You know how he stood by me."

"I know, and it was most gratifying,—not but that I feel sure you would have won without his aid. The old man simply couldn't quite be reconciled to her marrying in the army and living in Arizona."

"A strange land for a honey-moon certainly,—yet where and when was there a happier? Do you remember how the

Apaches jumped the Verde buck-board the very week after we were married?"

"And you spent half of the honey-moon scouting the Tonto Basin? I should say so! What with a courtship in a robbers' cave, a marriage in a cavalry camp, and a wedding tour in saddle, you had a unique experience, Wing, but—you deserved her." And Drummond turns and grips his comrade's hand.

Wing is silent a moment. His eyes are wistfully searching the elder's half-averted face.

"Jim, you told me awhile ago of your sister's approaching marriage. Are you not going on?"

"Yes. It will be early in October. She's blissfully happy is Puss, and he's a very substantial, solid sort of a fellow. I'm well content, at last, that her future is assured."

"And you are a free agent, practically. Isn't it time we heard of your own happiness,—your own vine and fig-tree, old man?"

"Time's gone by, I reckon," laughs Drummond, yet not merrily. "I've had too much to think of,—too much responsibility, and probably have lost my chance."

Wing looks as though he wanted mightily to say something, but conquers his impulse.

"October is a long way off," he finally remarks, "and I thought you might find earlier opportunity of going East. Now that Ned has entire charge of the business in Arizona the old gentleman takes life easier. The winter in Cuba did him a lot of good, and Fan writes that he seems so happy now, having his two girls and his little grandson under the same roof with his sister and her children. What a reunion after all these years!"

"Where are they living in Chicago?"

"You would know better than I, for—think of it!—I have never been east of the Missouri since my babyhood," answers Wing. "Fan writes that her aunt has a lovely house on what they call the North Side,—near the great water-works at the lake front."

"I know the neighborhood well," says Drummond. "Chicago is as familiar to me as San Francisco was to you. Only—I have no roof to call my own anywhere, and as soon as Puss is married shall not have a relative or friend on earth who is not much more deeply interested in somebody else." And the senior lieutenant is lying on his back now, blinking up at the rapidly scudding clouds. Presently he pulls the broad brim of his campaign hat down over his eyes. "What do you hear from your mother, Wing?"

"Nothing new. Bless the dear old lady! You should have seen her happiness in Harvey. She could hardly bear to let the little fellow out of her arms, and how she cried and clung to him when we parted at the Oakland wharf! Poor little mother! She has never given up the hope of seeing that scapegrace of an uncle of mine again."

"Has she ever heard how he tried to murder his nephew?" queries Drummond, grimly.

"Never. Nor have we the faintest trace of him since the break up of the old Morales gang at Fronteras. They went all to pieces after their encounter with you and 'C' troop. What a chain of disasters! Lost their leaders and three of their best men, lost their rendezvous at Moreno's, lost horses and mules,—for what our men didn't get the Apaches did,—and won absolutely nothing except the twenty-four-hour possession of a safe they hadn't time to open. Whereas I got my commission and my wife; Feeny, honorable wounds and mention and the chevrons of a first sergeant; Costigan got his sergeant's stripes and the medal of honor, Murphy his sergeantcy, Walsh and Latham medals and corporalships; and the only fellow who didn't get a blessed thing but scars was the commanding lieutenant,—your worthy self,—thanks to wiseacres at Washington who say Indian fighting isn't war."

"Didn't I get a letter of thanks from the department commander?" grins Drummond. "What else could I expect?"

"What else?" is Wing's impulsive rejoinder. Then, as though mindful of some admonition, quieting at once and speaking in tone less suggestive. "Well, in your case I suppose you can be content with nothing, but bless me if I could." Then, suddenly rising and respectfully touching his weather-beaten hat, he salutes a stoutly-built, soldierly-looking man in rough scouting dress, whose only badge of rank is the tarnished shoulder-strap with the silver leaf on the shabbiest old fatigue-coat to be found in the battalion, most of whose members, however, wear no coat at all.

"Hullo, Wing!—didn't mean to disturb your *siesta*,—Drummond here?" says the commander in his off-hand way, and at sound of the well-known voice Drummond, too, is on his feet in a twinkling.

"Seen the papers that came in to-day?" queries the colonel, obliterating from his sentences all verbal superfluities.

"Not yet, sir; any news?"

"Hell to pay in Chicago, so far as heard from. The railway strike has taken firm hold there. Police and militia both seem unable to do anything against the mob, and the authorities are stampeded. Your home, isn't it?"

"It was once, sir, but that was many a long year ago."

"W-e-ell," says the colonel, reflectively, stroking his grizzled beard, "it's my belief there is worse to come. It isn't the striking railway hands that will do the mischief, but every time there's a strike all the thieves and thugs and blackguards in the community turn out. That's what happened in Pittsburg,—that's what's the matter in Chicago. It looks to me as though the plea for regular troops would have to be granted."

"Think we can get there, sir?" asks Wing, eagerly.

"Can't say. We're supposed to have our hands full covering this section of Nebraska, though I haven't heard of a hostile Sioux this summer. Besides, they have full regiments of infantry at Omaha and along the lakes. Doesn't Mrs. Wing say anything about the trouble?"

"Her letter is four days old, sir, and only says her father looks upon the situation as one of much gravity; but women rarely see troubles of this kind until they come to their doors."

"Well, this is the *Times* of two days ago. It reached Sidney at breakfast-time this morning, and Hatton brought two or three copies out when he came with the mail. I thought you two might be interested." And with that the colonel goes strolling along down the bank of the stream, pausing here and there to chat with some officers or give some order relative to the grazing of the horses,—one of his especial "fads."

And this evening, just as the sun disappears over the low bluff line to the west and the horses are being picketed for the night, while from a score of cook-fires the appetizing savor of antelope-steak and the aroma of "soldier coffee" rise upon the air, a little dust-cloud sweeps out from the ravine into which disappears the Sidney road and comes floating out across the prairie. Keen-eyed troopers quickly note the speed with which it travels towards them. Officers and men, who have just been looking to the security of their steeds, pause now on their way to supper and stand gazing through the gloaming at the coming cloud. In five minutes the cause is apparent,—two swift riders, urging their horses to full speed, racing for the ford. Five minutes more and the foremost throws himself from saddle in the midst of the group at the colonel's tent and hands that officer a telegraphic despatch, which is received, opened, read with imperturbable gravity, and pocketed. To the manifest chagrin of the courier and disappointment of his officers, the colonel simply says,—

"W-e-ell, I'm going to supper. You all'd better have yours too."

"Why, blame his old hide!" pants the courier later, "the quartermaster told me never to lose a second, but git that to him before dark. The hull outfit's ordered to Chicago by special train."

And so, finding the secret out, the colonel presently puts aside professional *sang-froid* and condescends to be human again.

"Get a hearty supper all round, gentlemen, then—'boots and saddles' and away for Sidney!"

Two days later. A fierce July sun is pouring down a flood of humid, moisture-laden heat upon a densely-packed, sweltering mass of turbulent men, many of them flushed with drink, all of them flushed with triumph, for the ill-armed, ill-disciplined militia of the seventies—a pygmy force as compared with the expert "Guardsmen" of to-day—has been scattered to the winds: the sturdy police have been swept from the streets and driven to the shelter of the stations. Mob law rules supreme. Dense clouds of smoke are rising from sacked and ruined warehouses and from long trains of burning cars. Here and there little groups of striking employes have gathered, holding aloof from the reckless and infuriated mob, appalled at the sight of riot and devastation resulting from their ill-advised action. Many of their number, conscious of their responsibility for the scenes of bloodshed and pillage and wanton destruction of property, public and private, would now gladly undo their work and array themselves among the few defenders of the great corporations they have served for years and deserted at the call of leaders whom they never saw and in a cause they never understood, but there can be "no footsteps backward" now. The tide of riot has engulfed the great city of the West, and the majesty of the law is but the laughing-stock of the lowest of the masses. Huddled in their precinct stations the police are bandaging their bruised and broken heads. Rallied at their armories, the more determined of the militia are preparing to defend them and their colors against the anticipated attack of fifty times their force in "toughs,"—Chicago's vast accumulation of outlawed, vagabond, or criminal men. The city fathers are well-nigh hopeless. Merchants and business-men gather on 'Change with blanched faces and the oft-repeated query, "What next? What next?" Every moment brings tidings of fresh dismay. New fires, and a crippled and helpless department, for the rioters slash their hose and laugh their efforts to scorn. A gleam of hope shone in at ten o'clock, and the Board-room rang with cheers at the president's announcement that the regulars were coming,—a whole regiment of infantry from Omaha was already more than half-way. But the gleam died out at noon when, with white lips, an official read the telegram saying the strikers had "side-tracked" the special trains bearing the soldiers and they could not advance another mile.

And so they had on one road, but there are others, better guarded, better run. The sun is well over to the west again, Chicago is resigning itself to another night of horror, when from the suburbs there comes gliding in to the heart of the city the oddest-looking railway train that has been seen for years: a sight at which a host of riotous men break away from the threatening front, dragging with them those "pals" whom drink has either maddened or stupefied; a sight at which skulking blackguards who have picked up paving-stones drop them into the gutters and think twice before they lay hand on their revolver butts. No puffing engine hauls the train: the motor-power is at the rear. First and foremost is a platform car,—open, uncovered, but over its buffer glisten the barrels of the dreaded Gatling gun, and around the gun— can these be soldiers? Covered with dust and cinders, hardly a vestige of uniform among them, in the shabbiest of old felt hats, in hunting-shirts of flannel or buckskin, in scout-worn trousers and Indian leggings, but with their prairie-belts crammed with copper cartridges, their brawny brown hands grasping the browner carbine, their keen eyes peering straight into the faces of the thronging crowd, their bronze features set and stern, the whole car fairly bristles with men who have fought tribe after tribe of savage foes from the Yellowstone to the Sonora line, and who hold a savage mob in utter contempt. Here by the hub of the Gatling's wheel stands old Feeny, close at the elbow of dark-faced Drummond. "C" troop's first platoon "mans" the Gatling gun, and under its old leader of the Arizona campaigns "leads the procession" into the "Garden City" of the ante-bellum days. By Drummond's side is a railway official gazing ahead to see

Charles King

that every switch is properly set and signalling back to the engineer when to "slow," when to come confidently ahead. Behind the platform car come ordinary baggage and passenger coaches, black with men in the same rough, devil-may-care scouting rig. All but their horses and horse equipments left with the quartermaster at the Sidney station, the battalion has been run to Chicago exactly as it came from the plains, and Chicago's "toughs," who would have hooted and jeered, perhaps, at sight of polished brasses and natty uniforms, recoil bewildered before this gang of silent and disciplined "jay-hawkers." Steadily, silently, ominously, the train rolls along. As it is rounding a curve several ugly-looking fellows are seen running at speed towards the switch-lever at the next street-crossing. Excitedly the railway man clutches Drummond's elbow and points. Two troopers are kneeling close at hand.

"Shoot if they touch that switch," says Drummond, and instantly the locks click as the hammers are brought to full cock. The foremost runner is almost at the iron stand; his hand is outstretched to grasp it when a gasping, warning cry reaches his ears; glancing back he sees his fellows scattering to either side, and one look at the smooth rolling car reveals the cause: two carbines are levelled at him, and flat he throws himself on his face and rolls to one side amid derisive laughter from the strikers themselves. A little farther on a knot of surly rioters are gathered on the track. No warning whistle sounds and the clanging bell is too far to the rear to attract their attention. "Out of the way there!" is the blunt, roughly-spoken order. No time this for standing on ceremony. Vengeful and scowling the men spring aside, some stooping to pick up rocks, others reaching into their pockets for the ready pistol; but rocks are dropped and pistols undrawn as the train whirls rapidly by, and wrath gives place to mystification. Who—what are these strange, silent, stubbly-bearded, sun-tanned fellows in slouch hats, flannel shirts, and the worn old black belts over the shoulder? Even the engine has its guard, and half a dozen of them, perched upon the tender, have levelled their carbines to flank and rear, ready to let drive into the crowd the instant a brick is heaved or a trigger pulled.

And so into the great stone station they roll, and here they find the platforms jammed with citizens,—some drawn by curiosity, some active sympathizers in the strike, and many of them prominent leaders of the mob surging in the crowded thoroughfare without. The train has hardly come to a stand when from every direction the mass of outsiders is heaving up around it.

"Now, Feeny, clear the platform to the left. Take the other side, Wing," says Drummond, quietly, to the officer at the front door of the next car.

In the very fraction of a second the first sergeant and a dozen men have leaped from the deck, and straight into the heart of the crowd they go. "Back with ye! Out o' this!" are the stern, determined orders, emphasized by vigorous prods with the heavy carbine butts. Astonished at methods so prompt and decided, there is only such resistance as the weight and bulk of those in rear can offer, and that is but momentary. The sight of those gleaming Gatling barrels, the stern, brief orders and the rapid, confident advance combine to overcome all idea of resistance. On both sides, at the head of the train, the huge crowd, half laughing, half suffocating, is heaved back upon itself and sent like a great human wave rolling up to the iron lattice at the office end. Meantime, without an instant's delay the battalion springs out from the cars, forms ranks on the north platform, counts fours, and then, arms at right shoulder, away it goes with swinging, steady tramp around the rear of its train, across the parallel rows of rails, and in another moment, greeted by tremendous cheers from the occupants of long lines and high tiers of stores, offices, business blocks, the grimy, dusty, war-worn campaigners come striding down the crowded street. Heavens! how the people shout! Staid old burghers, portly business-men, trot panting alongside waving their hats and cheering themselves hoarse. "Them fellers hasn't no *bo*quets in their guns," is the way a street *gamin* expresses it.

"Whither are they going?"—"What have they first to do?" is the cry. Police officials ride now with the captain temporarily in command: a carriage has whisked the colonel over to head-quarters, but haste! haste! is the word. On they go, silent, grim, with the alkali dust of the North Platte crossing still coating their rusty garb. A great swing bridge looms ahead: a dozen police deploy on either side and check the attending crowd. Over they go at route step, and then, turning to the right, tramp on down a roughly-paved street, growing dim and dimmer every minute with stifling smoke. Presently they are crossing snake-like lines of hose, gashed and useless; passing fire apparatus standing unhitched and neglected; passing firemen exhausted and listless. Then occasional squads of scowling men give way before their steady tramp and are driven down alley-ways and around street-corners by reviving police. Then the head of column turns to the left and comes full upon a scene of tumult,—a great building in flames, a great mob surging about it defying police interference and bent apparently on gutting the structure from roof to cellar and pillaging the neighboring stores. Now, men of the—th, here's work cut out for you! Drive that mob! bloodlessly if you can, bloodletting if you must!

The colonel is again at the head. All are on foot. "Left front into line, double time;" the first company throws its long double rank from curb to curb, Drummond, its commander, striding at its front; Wing, his subaltern, anxiously watching him from among the file-closers. Already they have reached the rearmost of the rioting groups and, with warning cries and imprecations, these are scurrying to either side and falling into the hands of the accompanying police. Thicker, denser grows the smoke; thicker, denser the mob.

"Clear this street! Out of the way!" are the orders, and for a half-block or so clear it is. Then comes the first opposition. On a pile of lumber a tall, stalwart man in grizzled beard and slouching hatevidently a leader of mark among the mob—is shouting orders and encouragement. What he says cannot be heard, but now, tightly wedged between the rows of buildings, the mob is at bay, and, yelling mad response to the frantic appeals and gesticulations of their leader, at least two thousand reckless and infuriated men have faced the little battalion surging steadily up the narrow street.

"You may have to fire, Drummond," says the colonel, coolly. "Get in rear of your company." Obedient, the tall lieutenant turns and follows his chief along the front of his advancing line so as to pass around the flank. He is not fifty paces from the pile on which the mob leader, with half a dozen half-drunken satellites, is shouting his exhortations. Just as the lieutenant's arm is grazing grim old Feeny's elbow as he passes the first sergeant's station a brick comes hurtling through the air, strikes full upon the back of the officer's unprotected head, and sends him, face forward, into the muddy street. In the yell of triumph that follows, Wing's voice for an instant is unheard. Obedient to its principle, "Never load until about to fire," the battalion's carbines are still empty, but all on a sudden "C" troop halts. "With ball cartridges *load*!" is Wing's hoarse, stern order. "Now aim low when I give the word. *Fire by company. Company,* READY!" and, like one, the hammers click. But no command "Aim" follows. "Look out! Look out!—For God's sake don't fire! Out of the way!" are the frantic yells from the throats of the mob. Away they go. Scattering down side streets, alley-ways, behind lumber-piles, everywhere—anywhere. Many even throw themselves flat on their faces to escape the expected tempest of lead. "Don't fire," says the colonel, mercifully. "Forward, double time, and give them the butt. We'll support you." Down from the lumber-piles come the erstwhile truculent leaders. "Draw cartridge, men," orders Wing in wrath and disappointment. "Now, butts to the front, and give them hell. *Forward!*" And out he leaps to take the lead, dashing straight into the thick of the scattering mob, his men after him. There is a minute of wild yelling, cursing, of resounding blows and trampling feet, and in the midst of it all a single shot, and when Wing, breathless, is finally halted two squares farther on, only a dozen broken-headed wretches remain along the street to represent the furious mob that confronted them a few minutes before. Only these few and one writhing, bleeding form, around which half a dozen policemen are curiously gathered, and at whose side the battalion surgeon has just knelt.

"He's shot through and through," is his verdict, presently. "No power can save him. Who is he?"

"About the worst and most dangerous ringleader of riot this town has known, sir," is the answer of one of the police officials. "No one knew where he came from either—or his real name."

And then in his dying agony the fallen demagogue turns, and the other side of his twitching face comes uppermost. Even through the thin, grizzly beard there is plainly seen an ugly, jagged scar stretching from ear to chin.

"This isn't his first row by any manner of means, if it is his last," says a sergeant of police. "Look at that! Who shot him, anyhow?"

"I did," is the cool, prompt answer, and Sergeant Feeny raises his hand to his carried carbine and stands attention as he sees the surgeon kneeling there. "I did, and just in the nick of time. He had drawn a bead on our lieutenant; but even if he hadn't I'd have downed him, and so would any man in that company yonder." And Feeny points to where "C" troop stands resting after its charge.

"You knew him, then?"

"Knew him instantly, as a deserter, thafe, highway-man, and murderer,—knew him as Private Bland in Arizona, and would know him anywhere by that scar."

A policeman bends and wrenches a loaded revolver from the clutching, quivering fingers just as Wing comes striding back and shoulders a way into the group.

"Is he badly hurt, doctor? That was an awful whack."

"It isn't the lieutenant, sir," says Feeny, respectfully, but with strange significance in his tone as he draws a policeman aside. "Look!"

And Wing, bending over, gives one glance into the dying face, then covers his eyes with his hands and turns blindly, dizzily, away.

That evening a host of citizens are gathered about the bivouac of the battalion at the water-works while the trumpets are sounding tattoo. A few squares away the familiar notes come floating in through the open windows of a room where Jim Drummond is lying on a most comfortable sofa, which has been rolled close to the casement, where every whiff of the cool lake breeze can fan his face, and where, glancing languidly around, he contrasts the luxury of these surroundings with the rude simplicity of the life he has lived and loved so many years. Gray-haired George Harvey, kindly Mrs. Stone, his sister, blissful, beautiful Fanny Wing with burly baby Harvey in her arms and her proud, soldierly husband by her side, and a tall, lovely, silent girl have all been there to minister to his needs and bid him thrice welcome and make him feel that here, if anywhere on earth, he is at home. And here the battalion surgeon and the family physician unite in declaring he must remain until released by their order, and here for three days and nights he is nursed and petted and made so much of that he is unable to recognize himself, and here sister Puss comes to cry over and kiss and bless him and, in her turn, to be made much of and forbidden to leave, and then, after her big brother's return to duty with the battalion, now being fed and *feted* by all the North Side, he must needs come over every evening to see her; and, now that presentable uniforms have arrived and the rough beards have been shaved and the men of the old regiment look less like "toughs," but no more like American soldiers as our soldiers look in the field of their sternest service, her sisterly pride in her big brother is beautiful to see,—so is her self-abnegation, for, somehow or other, though he comes to see her he stays to look at Ruth Harvey, shy, silent, and beautiful, and soon, as though by common consent, that corner of the big parlor is given up to those two, the tall, stalwart trooper and the slender, willowy girl. And one evening he comes earlier than usual in manifest discomposure, and soon it transpires that important orders have reached him. Fanny turns pale. "Are you—all—ordered back?" she cries, and is for an instant radiant at his assurance that the order involves only himself. He is called to department head-quarters to report in person to the general commanding, who is about to make a tour through the mountains in Northwestern Wyoming and wants Drummond with the escort. She is radiant only until she catches sight of her sister's face. It is not so very warm an evening, yet she marshals the household out on the steps, out on the back veranda,—anywhere out of that parlor, where, just as the faint notes of the trumpets are heard, sounding their martial "tattoo," and just as Lieutenant Wing, returning from a tiptoed visit to his sleeping boy and escaped for the moment from the vigilance of his wife, now happens to go blundering in,—there is heard from the dimly-lighted corner near the piano the sound of subdued sobbing, the sound of a deep, manly voice, low, soothing, wondrously happy, the sound—a sound—indescribable in appropriate English, yet never misunderstood,—a sound at which Wing halts short, pauses one instant irresolute; then faces about and goes tip-toeing out into the brilliant sheen of the vestibule lamps,—into the brilliant gleam of his fond wife's questioning, reproachful eyes.

And for all answer, it being perhaps too public a spot for other demonstration, Wing simply hugs himself.

That night, under the arching roof of the great railway station, the comrades, so long united by the ties of such respect and affection as are engendered only by years of danger and hardship borne in common, and now so happily united by a closer tie, are pacing the platform absorbed in parting words.

"Jim, think what a load I've had to carry all these five years and forbidden by my good angel to breathe a word of it to you."

"I can't realize my own happiness, old man. I never dreamed that, after she got out into the world and saw for herself, that she would remember her girlish fancy or have another thought for me."

"I know you didn't. Yet Fan says that ever since the voyage

in the 'Newbern' little Ruth has never had a thought for anybody else."

There is a moment's silence, then Wing speaks again:

"There has not been time for mother's letter to reach me. I had to write, of course, and tell her of the fate that at last befell him. Do you know I feel as though after all it was my hand that did it."

"How so?"

"Feeny says he knew him the instant that side of his face was turned towards him,—the side my knife laid open years ago. That was a fatal scar."

THE END

Choose from Thousands of 1stWorldLibrary Classics By

A. M. Barnard
Ada Leverson
Adolphus William Ward
Aesop
Agatha Christie
Alexander Aaronsohn
Alexander Kielland
Alexandre Dumas
Alfred Gatty
Alfred Ollivant
Alice Duer Miller
Alice Turner Curtis
Alice Dunbar
Allen Chapman
Alleyne Ireland
Ambrose Bierce
Amelia E. Barr
Amory H. Bradford
Andrew Lang
Andrew McFarland Davis
Andy Adams
Angela Brazil
Anna Alice Chapin
Anna Sewell
Annie Besant
Annie Hamilton Donnell
Annie Payson Call
Annie Roe Carr
Annonaymous
Anton Chekhov
Archibald Lee Fletcher
Arnold Bennett
Arthur C. Benson
Arthur Conan Doyle
Arthur M. Winfield
Arthur Ransome
Arthur Schnitzler
Arthur Train
Atticus
B.H. Baden-Powell
B. M. Bower
B. C. Chatterjee
Baroness Emmuska Orczy
Baroness Orczy
Basil King
Bayard Taylor
Ben Macomber
Bertha Muzzy Bower
Bjornstjerne Bjornson

Booth Tarkington
Boyd Cable
Bram Stoker
C. Collodi
C. E. Orr
C. M. Ingleby
Carolyn Wells
Catherine Parr Traill
Charles A. Eastman
Charles Amory Beach
Charles Dickens
Charles Dudley Warner
Charles Farrar Browne
Charles Ives
Charles Kingsley
Charles Klein
Charles Hanson Towne
Charles Lathrop Pack
Charles Romyn Dake
Charles Whibley
Charles Willing Beale
Charlotte M. Braeme
Charlotte M. Yonge
Charlotte Perkins Stetson
Clair W. Hayes
Clarence Day Jr.
Clarence E. Mulford
Clemence Housman
Confucius
Coningsby Dawson
Cornelis DeWitt Wilcox
Cyril Burleigh
D. H. Lawrence
Daniel Defoe
David Garnett
Dinah Craik
Don Carlos Janes
Donald Keyhoe
Dorothy Kilner
Dougan Clark
Douglas Fairbanks
E. Nesbit
E. P. Roe
E. Phillips Oppenheim
E. S. Brooks
Earl Barnes
Edgar Rice Burroughs
Edith Van Dyne
Edith Wharton

Edward Everett Hale
Edward J. O'Biren
Edward S. Ellis
Edwin L. Arnold
Eleanor Atkins
Eleanor Hallowell Abbott
Eliot Gregory
Elizabeth Gaskell
Elizabeth McCracken
Elizabeth Von Arnim
Ellem Key
Emerson Hough
Emilie F. Carlen
Emily Bronte
Emily Dickinson
Enid Bagnold
Enilor Macartney Lane
Erasmus W. Jones
Ernie Howard Pie
Ethel May Dell
Ethel Turner
Ethel Watts Mumford
Eugene Sue
Eugenie Foa
Eugene Wood
Eustace Hale Ball
Evelyn Everett-green
Everard Cotes
F. H. Cheley
F. J. Cross
F. Marion Crawford
Fannie E. Newberry
Federick Austin Ogg
Ferdinand Ossendowski
Fergus Hume
Florence A. Kilpatrick
Fremont B. Deering
Francis Bacon
Francis Darwin
Frances Hodgson Burnett
Frances Parkinson Keyes
Frank Gee Patchin
Frank Harris
Frank Jewett Mather
Frank L. Packard
Frank V. Webster
Frederic Stewart Isham
Frederick Trevor Hill
Frederick Winslow Taylor

Friedrich Kerst	Hayden Carruth	James Branch Cabell
Friedrich Nietzsche	Helent Hunt Jackson	James DeMille
Fyodor Dostoyevsky	Helen Nicolay	James Joyce
G.A. Henty	Hendrik Conscience	James Lane Allen
G.K. Chesterton	Hendy David Thoreau	James Lane Allen
Gabrielle E. Jackson	Henri Barbusse	James Oliver Curwood
Garrett P. Serviss	Henrik Ibsen	James Oppenheim
Gaston Leroux	Henry Adams	James Otis
George A. Warren	Henry Ford	James R. Driscoll
George Ade	Henry Frost	Jane Abbott
Geroge Bernard Shaw	Henry James	Jane Austen
George Cary Eggleston	Henry Jones Ford	Jane L. Stewart
George Durston	Henry Seton Merriman	Janet Aldridge
George Ebers	Henry W Longfellow	Jens Peter Jacobsen
George Eliot	Herbert A. Giles	Jerome K. Jerome
George Gissing	Herbert Carter	Jessie Graham Flower
George MacDonald	Herbert N. Casson	John Buchan
George Meredith	Herman Hesse	John Burroughs
George Orwell	Hildegard G. Frey	John Cournos
George Sylvester Viereck	Homer	John F. Kennedy
George Tucker	Honore De Balzac	John Gay
George W. Cable	Horace B. Day	John Glasworthy
George Wharton James	Horace Walpole	John Habberton
Gertrude Atherton	Horatio Alger Jr.	John Joy Bell
Gordon Casserly	Howard Pyle	John Kendrick Bangs
Grace E. King	Howard R. Garis	John Milton
Grace Gallatin	Hugh Lofting	John Philip Sousa
Grace Greenwood	Hugh Walpole	John Taintor Foote
Grant Allen	Humphry Ward	Jonas Lauritz Idemil Lie
Guillermo A. Sherwell	Ian Maclaren	Jonathan Swift
Gulielma Zollinger	Inez Haynes Gillmore	Joseph A. Altsheler
Gustav Flaubert	Irving Bacheller	Joseph Carey
H. A. Cody	Isabel Cecilia Williams	Joseph Conrad
H. B. Irving	Isabel Hornibrook	Joseph E. Badger Jr
H.C. Bailey	Israel Abrahams	Joseph Hergesheimer
H. G. Wells	Ivan Turgenev	Joseph Jacobs
H. H. Munro	J.G.Austin	Jules Vernes
H. Irving Hancock	J. Henri Fabre	Julian Hawthrone
H. R. Naylor	J. M. Barrie	Julie A Lippmann
H Rider Haggard	J. M. Walsh	Justin Huntly McCarthy
H. W. C. Davis	J. Macdonald Oxley	Kakuzo Okakura
Ealdeman Julius	J. R. Miller	Karle Wilson Baker
Hall Caine	J. S. Fletcher	Kate Chopin
Hamilton Wright Mabie	J. S. Knowles	Kenneth Grahame
Hans Christian Andersen	J. Storer Clouston	Kenneth McGaffey
Harold Avery	J. W. Duffield	Kate Langley Bosher
Harold McGrath	Jack London	Kate Langley Bosher
Harriet Beecher Stowe	Jacob Abbott	Katherine Cecil Thurston
Harry Castlemon	James Allen	Katherine Stokes
Harry Coghill	James Andrews	L. A. Abbot
Harry Houidini	James Baldwin	L. T. Meade

L. Frank Baum
Latta Griswold
Laura Dent Crane
Laura Lee Hope
Laurence Housman
Lawrence Beasley
Leo Tolstoy
Leonid Andreyev
Lewis Carroll
Lewis Sperry Chafer
Lilian Bell
Lloyd Osbourne
Louis Hughes
Louis Joseph Vance
Louis Tracy
Louisa May Alcott
Lucy Fitch Perkins
Lucy Maud Montgomery
Luther Benson
Lydia Miller Middleton
Lyndon Orr
M. Corvus
M. H. Adams
Margaret E. Sangster
Margret Howth
Margaret Vandercook
Margaret W. Hungerford
Margret Penrose
Maria Edgeworth
Maria Thompson Daviess
Mariano Azuela
Marion Polk Angellotti
Mark Overton
Mark Twain
Mary Austin
Mary Catherine Crowley
Mary Cole
Mary Hastings Bradley
Mary Roberts Rinehart
Mary Rowlandson
M. Wollstonecraft Shelley
Maud Lindsay
Max Beerbohm
Myra Kelly
Nathaniel Hawthrone
Nicolo Machiavelli
O. F. Walton
Oscar Wilde

Owen Johnson
P.G. Wodehouse
Paul and Mabel Thorne
Paul G. Tomlinson
Paul Severing
Percy Brebner
Percy Keese Fitzhugh
Peter B. Kyne
Plato
Quincy Allen
R. Derby Holmes
R. L. Stevenson
R. S. Ball
Rabindranath Tagore
Rahul Alvares
Ralph Bonehill
Ralph Henry Barbour
Ralph Victor
Ralph Waldo Emmerson
Rene Descartes
Ray Cummings
Rex Beach
Rex E. Beach
Richard Harding Davis
Richard Jefferies
Richard Le Gallienne
Robert Barr
Robert Frost
Robert Gordon Anderson
Robert L. Drake
Robert Lansing
Robert Lynd
Robert Michael Ballantyne
Robert W. Chambers
Rosa Nouchette Carey
Rudyard Kipling
Saint Augustine
Samuel B. Allison
Samuel Hopkins Adams
Sarah Bernhardt
Sarah C. Hallowell
Selma Lagerlof
Sherwood Anderson
Sigmund Freud
Standish O'Grady
Stanley Weyman
Stella Benson
Stella M. Francis

Stephen Crane
Stewart Edward White
Stijn Streuvels
Swami Abhedananda
Swami Parmananda
T. S. Ackland
T. S. Arthur
The Princess Der Ling
Thomas A. Janvier
Thomas A Kempis
Thomas Anderton
Thomas Bailey Aldrich
Thomas Bulfinch
Thomas De Quincey
Thomas Dixon
Thomas H. Huxley
Thomas Hardy
Thomas More
Thornton W. Burgess
U. S. Grant
Upton Sinclair
Valentine Williams
Various Authors
Vaughan Kester
Victor Appleton
Victor G. Durham
Victoria Cross
Virginia Woolf
Wadsworth Camp
Walter Camp
Walter Scott
Washington Irving
Wilbur Lawton
Wilkie Collins
Willa Cather
Willard F. Baker
William Dean Howells
William le Queux
W. Makepeace Thackeray
William W. Walter
William Shakespeare
Winston Churchill
Yei Theodora Ozaki
Yogi Ramacharaka
Young E. Allison
Zane Grey

www.ingramcontent.com/pod-product-compliance
Lightning Source LLC
Chambersburg PA
CBHW030316180626
46810CB00003B/1100